BEYOND THE IRON™

A Training Guide for Ultra-Distance Triathlons

BY WAYNE KURTZ

The information contained in this book is intended to be educational and not for diagnosis, prescription, or treatment of any health disorder whatsoever. This book is sold with the understanding that neither the author nor publisher is engaged in rendering any legal, psychological, or accounting advice. The publisher and author disclaim personal liability, directly or indirectly, for advice of information presented within. Although the author and publisher have prepared this manuscript with utmost care and diligence and have made every effort to ensure the accuracy and completeness of the information contained within, we assume no responsibility for errors, inaccuracies, omissions or inconsistencies.

Library of Congress Control Number: 2010943408

ISBN–13: 9780615436548

Beyond The Iron soft–cover edition 2010

Printed in the United States of America

Design by Erin Pace-Molina.

Cover photo by Gail Shoop-Lamy.

For more information about special discounts for bulk purchases, please contact 3L Publishing at 916.300.8012 or log onto our website at www.3LPublishing.com.

TESTIMONIALS

"Once you've run a marathon (or two), you start seeing things in a different perspective. What if ...? You get curious and motivated ... Wayne's book gives you lots of useful ideas, tips and good advice. After reading it you will feel like jumping into your sports gear and heading for your training in hope to reach your ultimate goal."
▪ Judit Kulcsar, International Marketing and PR Manager, Budapest Marathon Organisation

"There is a quote that goes something like this: 'If God invented marathons to keep people from doing anything more stupid, then triathlons must have taken him by complete surprise.' I have heard this quote almost from the beginning of my running career and always found it funny.

However, for as long as I had heard it, it felt outdated. You see, just the race I ever did of any note as an adult was a 12-hour race around a one-mile loop. I soon found there were tons of people taking God by complete surprise.

The marathon is quickly becoming the training run for many athletes as the springboard to ultra events. Multiple-day triathlons, while not the norm, are far more commonplace than one would think logic would dictate. As such, those people who are looking to take on the next ultimate challenge, which are growing in number each day, need a handbook that takes them through how to prepare and train for those events. Wayne's book, *Beyond the Iron*, is that handbook. Filled with insight from a man who has accomplished what most can only dream, this is a book that should be on the training table of anyone hoping to go 'beyond.'"

- Dane Rauschenberg, extreme athlete, author and speaker for "See Dane Run"

"Today, the world's great adventurers look inward rather than outward for unexplored regions to conquer. Wayne Kurtz is such an adventurer, constantly chasing his own physical, emotional and spiritual capabilities to the very edge by tackling seemingly impossible feats of ultra-endurance. After years living in regions few dare explore, Wayne has returned with a map; this book is his invitation to view that map and chart the course to your own greatest adventure."

▪ Will Laughlin, record-setting ultra-distance runner and founder of Nutrients.com

"Straight forward and informative, yet not without the love — the passion that is the race ... *Beyond the Iron* is not only user friendly, but good-guy friendly — like having your best friend walk you through it."

▪ David Moreno, world-class yoga instructor, www.moryoga.com

"An awesome reference for anyone interested in ultra-endurance-based events! Wayne makes the thought of multiple iron distance events seem within reach for us all!"

▪ Ray Zahab, adventurer and founder of impossible2Possible

"Don't do an Ultra-Distance Triathlon before you've read this comprehensive, experience-based book. *Beyond The Iron* will save you from a lot of mistakes and double your confidence of a successful finish."
▪ Matt Fitzgerald, senior writer/editor, Competitor Group, Inc.

"Wayne knows the true pulse of the ultra-distance industry. *Beyond the Iron* is a must-read for athletes who are looking, training for, and competing in ultra-distance races. This book offers a complete training program and advice to getting into and through some of the world's most challenging ultra-distance events. As a trusted colleague, I value his advice and wisdom and look forward to seeing more of Wayne in the news and in the record books. From the marathoner looking for the next distance challenge to the experience ultra-distance racer, this book must be on your book shelf!"
▪ Alix Shutello, publisher, *Runners Illustrated*, www.runnersillustrated.com

"Ultra triathlons have always been a bit of a mystery for triathletes. Here Wayne Kurtz unravels the mystery and helps you get on-track for going really long."
▪ Joe Friel, coach and author, *Triathlete's Training Bible*

"As an ultra-endurance athlete, coach and sport psychology consultant I'm intimate with the importance of building confidence through knowledge when taking on a new race project or wanting to up the ante in your existing program. By offering the intricate ins and outs of how to get to the start line of your chosen endurance endeavor, *Beyond the Iron* is an excellent launching point in building optimal confidence-building preparation. Thanks, Wayne, for offering this important book!"
▪ Terri Schneider, www.terrischneider.net

"Any individual looking to test their boundaries in the world of ultras, first needs to have the knowledge and support of a dedicated and passionate expert that has been through it. Wayne Kurtz is that man for you and his book, *Beyond the Iron* should be your bible."
▪ Graeme Street, creator of Cyclo-CORE Training, owner of Cyclo-CLUB.com and the host of the Everyday Cyclist Podcast

"For many athletes, a marathon or an Ironman Triathlon is the ultimate endurance event. But for some people those distances are just not enough. Wayne Kurtz's book uses his years of competitive success and lessons learned to present training and racing tips for those who seek to go beyond the Ironman Triathlon. In the book, Wayne presents the history of ultra triathlons, information on how to do on race day(s) including how to select gear, race strategies, and injury prevention and visualization techniques. The book provides a roadmap of about what to do, and what not to do, in your quest for the successful completion of an ultra triathlon."

▪ Joe Jurczyk, race director, Burning River 100-Mile Endurance Run and founder, ULTRA discussion group

"I first got to know Wayne in 2006 at the inaugural 24 Hours of Triathlon. His perpetually sunny disposition revealed that he loved what he was doing and was doing what he loved. This attitude pervaded the race and proved infectious. In my experience, these are qualities essential to long-term success at Ultra-Distance Triathlons, as I hope you will discover for yourself!"

▪ Ian Adamson, 7x Adventure Race World Champion, 3x Guinness World Record Holder for Endurance Kayaking, 3x Eco-Challenge Winner, ESPN X-Games Gold medalist, and author *Runner's World Guide to Adventure Racing*

"Have you ever wondered if you have what it takes to complete what is sure the ultimate test of endurance, the Ultra-Distance Triathlon? In this thought-provoking, well-written and extremely comprehensive bible on how to train and race the 'ultra' distance, author Wayne Kurtz shares his unique insights and experience in a book that is sure to help the aspiring ultra-distance racer. You'll learn how to deal with the enormous mental and physical demands of the distance — and enjoy the process!"

▪ Al Lyman, CSCS, FMS, creator of the functional strength and flexibility training system for runners-CORE (http://runner-core.com), and co-director of the Pursuit-Athletic-Performance Gait Analysis Lab. For more information, go to http://coach-al.com, or http://pursuit-athletic-performance.com

"Right out of the gates, Kurtz, lays down the groundwork for all of us who come to the point in our sporting career in which we ask the question, 'What's next?' He embarks on a journey that illustrates what challenges lay ahead of 'regular-distance' events, wrapping the imaginations, dreams and goals of athletes determined to push their own physical and mental boundaries in with his passion for enduring the thrill of outdoor pursuits. Kurtz eloquently guides us through the process of making the transition from competing in events that we consider the norm to greater distance and modified format; all the while maintaining an excitement for the same sports that got us all started. *Beyond the Iron* is a must-have guide for any athlete aspiring to achieve the mental fortitude and physical conditioning that will bring us to that next level."

▪ Joel Perrella, editor, *Breathe Magazine*
www.breathemag.ca

"Wayne and *Beyond The Iron* are both extraordinary. The talents, gifts and absolute grace make this book a journey we should all read and share. As a coach and endurance athlete myself, I have great respect, admiration and gratitude for Wayne and all he does to make the world a better place to live. Blessings!"

▪ Lisa Smith-Batchen
www.dreamchaserevents.com, www.runhope.com

"For the person entertaining the challenge of going beyond the Iron-Distance, you probably know what it means to make a game plan. Wayne has taken his extensive knowledge in the art of Ultra racing and passed it on in a concise format laced with some entertaining history about multi-sport. Because Wayne is able to refer to his own experiences, the reader is able to gain a perspective not achieved elsewhere, and hopefully learn from Wayne's own trials and tribulations. This is a must read for anyone preparing to step up to the next level."

- Dean Warhaft, Endurance Traveler

TABLE OF CONTENTS

DEDICATION

My passion for triathlons and endurance sports started in 1985 while in college. I was a swimmer by background and remember asking my mother when she came to visit me at college to drive out to a five-mile running course in the college town. I just decided to buy some New Balance running shoes (I only ran with sports not track or cross-country running) and that was the beginning. A few months later, I was home for a few days and was at the local golf course and saw an entry form for a triathlon in my hometown county park in Pittsburgh. So, after painting my grandmother's house and doing some other odd jobs, I saved up enough money for my Centurion Racing Bike. I still recall the conversation with my parents where I said, "Well now I have my bike, which is the major expense, and the majority of my costs are now gone."

Well, as we have seen over the last 25 years, new technology, time-trial bikes, mountain bikes, racing bikes, clip-less pedals, aero bars, aero wheels, wet-suits, so many pairs of running shoes, all the clothing for each season, etc. made my statement to my parents inaccurate to say the least! In my mind, however, spending the money, over the years, has been a worthwhile lifestyle investment — and triathlons have been my passion ever since.

My parents, sister and my lovely bride have a few classic quotes about me. Among them are: "Wayne beats to his own drum," and, "Was Wayne dropped on his head when he was a baby?" I hear this a lot now, especially with competing in Ultra-Distance Triathlons.

Twenty-five years later and hundreds of endurance races in many different sports, traveling all over North America and Europe, meeting lifelong friends has been an absolutely amazing experience. I still get nervous at the start of a marathon, ultra-running race, triathlon, snowshoe race, adventure race, cycling race, etc. — and that's what keeps it so fresh and fun for me.

I want to thank my mother for always believing in me when I came up with a new idea; my father for being there for all those years with all the sports (participating and, of course, watching my beloved Pittsburgh Steelers football team); and my sister for always asking me, "You have to be kidding me. What else are you going to come up with?" Finally Janice, my wife, best friend and Greek goddess and Super Crew for the best times of my life, our travels and races, Greek traditions, and our numerous Godchildren.

Of course a few others: my coach and great friend, Nate Llerandi for always challenging me with creating great workouts over all these years.

Finally, it has been such a great experience finding Michelle Gamble-Risley and 3L Publishing by reading an article on the plane in a magazine about how they are different from the normal publishing company. Thanks for keeping me on track and providing your creative ideas and expertise.

FOREWORD

By Dr. JoAnn Dahlkoetter

Congratulations! Your investment in Wayne Kurtz's book will offer substantial rewards in gaining the physical, mental and performance edge you need to stretch your goals and go *Beyond the Iron*, and go farther than you ever thought possible in your training and racing — and in your life.

Wayne Kurtz has written the ultimate book for athletic and personal success. This book is a gold mine — a wealth of information and inspiration to take you to the next level. Everyone needs this book — it's like having Wayne right here with you as your own personal coach.

Wayne Kurtz has a unique combination of success skills and sports experience unlike any professional

I've ever worked with. He is an incredible athlete with a brilliant mind. He understands exactly what athletes' need, and he knows how to get you to the finish line. I have tremendous respect for all of his amazing accomplishments.

I was drawn to the *Beyond the Iron* book because it offers a unique approach for people who are serious about challenging themselves in mind, body and spirit. Using Wayne's training system, you'll have peak performance strategies for every possible ultra event. You can develop a specific, customized plan of action to perform and feel your best in your training and racing when it really counts.

As an NBC-TV OLYMPICS expert guest, *Your Performing Edge* best-selling author, Stanford-trained sports psychologist, coach to OLYMPIC Gold Medalists, SF Marathon winner, and champion Ironman triathlete, I look to Wayne Kurtz as one of the finest consultants and coaches I've had the opportunity to partner with.

For more than 30 years, I have been coaching motivated athletes, entrepreneurs and corporate leaders with my *Your Performing Edge* techniques in how to energize their minds and bodies, focus and feel good, be healthier and fitter than ever, and perform their best when it counts the most.

When you're working with the intricate balance between body and mind — as it applies to high-level performance like an Ultra-Distance Triathlon — you want breakthrough strategies that are well constructed, time-tested and emanate from an authority you can trust. Wayne Kurtz has the leading-edge knowledge and "hands-on" experience to put you at the top of your game. Through his lifelong passion and extensive racing background in various endurance sport races throughout the world, he has been able to understand what really works and translate the information in this book into a meaningful approach that can benefit everyone.

Wayne has all the right ingredients to be your personal coach, through his book, and beyond. I had the opportunity to work with Wayne Kurtz in my coach certification program, Performing Edge Coaching International. Wayne is absolutely the best athlete and coach that I have had the chance to partner with. He has a deep understanding of the mental side of training, and he practices the principles he is teaching. He's an excellent coach and leader. He knows exactly what athletes need to learn because he is one. He is one of the most disciplined, creative, inspiring, individuals I've ever met. I have complete confidence in Wayne as your Performing Edge Coach, and I highly recommend his book to you if you want to aim higher and go *Beyond the Iron*.

Dr. JoAnn Dahlkoetter (www.DrJoAnn.com)
Best-selling author, *YOUR PERFORMING EDGE*
OLYMPIC Performance Edge Coach on OPRAH
and NBC OLYMPICS – TV Commentator

CEO of Performing Edge Coach International
Coach to CEO's and Olympic Gold Medalists
Winner, San Francisco Marathon
World Championship Hawaii Ironman Triathlon,
Champion athlete

#1 Triathlete in the U.S. by *Triathlete Magazine*, 1982,
Stanford University Medical Center Trained Sports
Psychologist

INTRODUCTION

If you've picked up this book, I am certain you're very aware of what the Ironman Triathlon is all about, so I won't spend time reviewing the aspects of training and racing for this race. So you may have done the Ironman Triathlon and the question is: What's next for a significant triathlon challenge? *Beyond the Iron* is written for those athletes interested in learning how to train for races beyond the Ironman distance — the Ultra-Distance Triathlons, which includes the Double Ultra-Distance Triathlon distance up to Deca Triathlon. I will provide an overview of what *Beyond the Iron* is designed to do and allow you get to know me a little bit, so you feel comfortable with my qualifications as your coach as we embark on this journey as a kindred team.

Beyond the Iron provides an in-depth overview of the types of events that take place around the world, offers specific training ideas/schedules, and helps you design a plan that meets your needs. Before you sign up, I want you to know this should be an interactive experience. You will not be able to successfully tackle the challenge of an Ultra-Distance Triathlon without commitment, goal setting, tenacity, and more importantly desire; but through the use of my training programs including the most important component — mental training — I hope to help you reach your goal and achieve your dream of triumphantly crossing the finish line. As I have experienced, these races are full of lifetime memories and life-changing experiences.

Before I launch into the details, I want to give you an introduction to my background as I guide you through this incredible mental and physical journey to help you successfully train for these exceptional triathlons. My name is Wayne Kurtz, and I am the founder of RaceTwitch.com (http://www.racetwitch.com), Endurance Racing Report (http://www.enduranceracingreport.com), and RacePeak.com (http://www.racepeak.com). I have a lifelong passion for racing in various endurance sport races throughout the world. I quite simply love this sport. In fact, I live for it, and it's part of my makeup.

Over the last 25 years, I have tested myself and triumphed over hundreds of endurance race events. I thrive on the adrenalin and feel an unparalleled passion about the challenge, strength and endurance required not just of the physical body but the test of my mental stamina to hang in there and confront all the obstacles. The thrill of the stick-to-it mentality to keep going even when I am physically exhausted, allowing my mind to take over, pushing to never give into physical defeat is why I am so passionate about this sport.

Yet I am not a man defined only by my dedication to the Ultra-Triathlon challenges. I love and appreciate all physical endurance and other athletic challenges, including ultra-running, cycling and snowshoe races at various distances and other long-distance endurance events. My recent focuses include the Double, Quintuple, Deca Triathlon, 100-mile and multi-day running events. My journey to learn how to properly train and prepare for these events continues to evolve each year. And now I am in the fortunate position to share some of this knowledge and insight with you — so you too can successfully train and prepare both mentally and physically to pursue your goals.

In preparing you for these events, I am going to give you a specific training plan and expertise that will apply to Ultra-Distance Triathlons. Also look for the Twitch Tips (RaceTwitch.com) that highlight key areas for each chapter. I understand that every athlete has his or her specific goals and reasons for attempting and racing in whatever event he or she chooses; but overall most would agree that the journey to the finish line is what resonates in most athletes' minds — and most certainly in mine.

Throughout all of my racing experiences and challenges, I've learned a lot. I've found out more about myself; I've traveled to some memorable places; I've bonded with and created lifelong friendships that will continue to touch and define my life. I've had the pleasure of meeting hundreds of athletes, race directors and others around the world where the sport has become a community for me. A place where I have dear friends and supporters I know I could count on for just about anything. If you're ready to train and prepare yourself for the mental and physical tests required to succeed at these Ultra-Distance Triathlon events, then please use *Beyond the Iron* to its fullest potential to help you achieve your goals.

- Wayne Kurtz

CHAPTER 1 – BREAKING BOUNDARIES: HISTORY OF THE RACES

"To give anything less than your best is to sacrifice the gift." ▪ Steve Prefontaine

Maybe you've done an Ironman Triathlon and perhaps you did exceptionally well or even won. You're ready to advance to a longer distance event; but at the same time, maybe you don't know what is that next level or you have only vaguely heard terms such as Ultraman or Double Ultra Triathlons — and you have little or no information about the events. You've possibly talked to a friend or two who has participated in one or two around the globe. Maybe they only shared their personal reflections about the race, but that is not enough for you. You want to get more information and try to attempt one of these longer distance races.

You may be highly interested and motivated to find out more, learn the best approaches to a training plan, and participate in an Ultra-Distance Triathlon. So, read on as I introduce Ultra-Distance Triathlons and a bit of history on the origin of these races.

From Triathlon to Ultra-Distance Triathlons

How exactly did these triathlons get started and why? What are these kinds of races designed to do in terms of challenge your strength and endurance and create unique tests for you as an athlete?

Early triathlons started with runners and endurance junkies seeking new ways to challenge themselves. Of course, the triathlon combined swimming, biking and running to create a unique challenge of running on tired legs. The first triathlons were held in 1974 at San Diego Mission Bay. Over time, triathlons evolved into what is now known as "Ironman Triathlon," which encompasses the aforementioned Ironman Triathlon and the annual Ironman World Championship that is famously held in Hawaii since 1978.

Yet Ironman athletes were not satisfied with the challenge of 2.4-miles swimming, 112-mile biking, and 26.2-mile-marathon competitions. So the early Ironman race design became the foundation or springboard if you will for the Ultra-Distance Triathlon races that emerged straight from the imaginations, dreams and goals of the athletes who were determined to find greater and greater challenges to test boundaries of their own physical and mental capabilities. These multi-sport events have actually developed from original Ironman Triathlon competitions into the Double Ultra Triathlon (since the Ironman is now a trademarked name, the races cannot be named Double Ironman and are normally titled Double Ultra Triathlon).

The very first Double Ultra Triathlon took place in 1984 in Huntsville, Alabama and consisted of 4.8-miles swimming, 224-miles biking, and 52.4-miles running, which is still considered today's standard for a Double Ultra Triathlon. Athletes from all over the world attended the first race that was scheduled over Labor Day of that year. Ray and Nancy Shephard directed that race and took over for a friend who bowed out. Since then, the race has grown and changed and become increasingly competitive, grueling and difficult to complete, and it attracts an estimated 20 to 30 athletes each year. The original race is now held in Virginia (Virginia hosts two races — a Double and Triple Ultra Triathlon).

The Governing Body and Races

The Double Ultra Triathlon spurred on the creation of ever-increasing challenges and eventually longer distance Ultra Triathlons, which is the focus of this book. The World Triathlon Corporation (WTC) organizes the large Ironman triathlons, which "is a for-profit corporation that organizes, promotes and licenses the Ironman Triathlon series of triathlon races. WTC is also the owner of numerous 'Ironman' and related trademarks used both in connection with the Ironman race series and in conjunction with various goods and services."

Standards and practices were required to create consistency and guidelines for Ultra-Distance Triathlons. Thus, a governing body now exists for Ultra-Distance Triathlons, called the International Ultra Triathlon Association (www.iutasport.com). The IUTA is the official governing body of the Ultra-Distance Triathlon, which is devoted to creating interest in the sport; developing the sport through increased athlete participation; and promoting sanctioned venues worldwide. The goal of the IUTA is to take the Ultra-Distance Triathlon to greater heights.

The IUTA's website contains updates and information about the races in the World Cup series. The World Cup races continue to expand each year.

As the sanctioning body of the races, the IUTA has responsibility and authority to promote the following race formats, which are also the most popular international IUTA race distance and include the following:

- **Double Triathlon** – 4.8-miles (7.6KM) swim, 224-mile (360KM) bike, 52.4-mile (84.4KM) run
- **Triple Triathlon** – 7.2-mile (11.4KM) swim, 336-mile (540KM) bike, 78.6-mile (126.6KM) run

These additional races are designed to push the thresholds of stamina and endurance to the extreme. Only an elite group of athletes participate in these races, which include the following series of races held annually in Mexico (November) (the Deca Triathlon would be considered the "Hawaii Ironman" of ultra-distance races):

- **Quadruple Triathlon** – 9.6-mile (15.2KM) swim, 448-mile (720KM) bike, 104-mile (168.8KM) run
- **Quintuple Triathlon** – 12-mile (19KM) swim, 560-mile (900KM) bike, 131-mile (211KM) run
- **Deca Triathlon** – 24-mile (38KM) swim, 1,120-mile (1,800KM) bike, 262-mile (422KM) run*
- **Double Deca Triathlon** – 48-mile (76KM) swim, 2,240-mile (3,600KM) bike, 524-mile (844KM) run

*The races held in Mexico change the format each year from a continuous race to an "Iron-man-distance-per-day" format. For example, the 2008 Deca Triathlon was continuous, thus 24 miles of swimming followed by 1,120 miles of biking and finishing with an "easy" 262 miles of running. The 2009 race was in the "one-Ironman-per-day-for-10-days format." Each race has its own difficulties with sleep deprivation for the continuous versus the recovery needed each day after sleeping in the per-day format.

Unique Experiences and Challenges

The original concept for the event has also attracted worldwide interest, with the format being primarily adopted in Europe and a Double/Triple Triathlon held in the United States in the state of Virginia (an additional Double Triathlon will be held in Tampa). Other Double Triathlon competitions have been held in Hungary, France, Slovenia, Austria and Mexico (as mentioned earlier) and many other locations.

As you look at Ultra-Distance Triathlons locations that range from Europe to Mexico, you realize that not all courses or races are created the same. Very similar to ultra-running, the Ultra-Distance Triathlon is evolving and gaining popularity. New competitors will be offered unique experiences and challenges dependent upon location, course and terrain, which all can impact the athlete's performance.

One thing to recognize about this group of endurance athletes: They are devoted to the idea of the ability to finish not necessarily to win — although winning is great and certainly the goal as well, but not the sole intention. I am personally passionate about the ability to strengthen, endure and bring the challenge to its completion regardless of where I fall into the final line up — be it first or second or even last; it doesn't matter as long as I confront and defy the challenge in its entirety.

Today, Ironman triathletes ready to take it to the next level are joining the growing ranks of those athletes who have accepted the Ultra-Distance

TWITCH TIPS

Check out IUTA website (http://www.iutasport.com) for more information of Ultra-Distance Triathlons held throughout the world.

Triathlon challenge and continue to pursue their dreams. Preparing to take on an Ultra-Distance Triathlon requires commitment, determination and intense training to get your mind, body and spirit prepared for the adventure.

In the next chapters, I will guide you through this training program and process, which will include all facets of training for these unique races. I will walk you through the required training, strategies to optimize your body/mind, and insights to help you cross the finish line with a sense of accomplishment, pride and satisfaction.

CHAPTER 2 – SPECIFIC RACE DISTANCES AND CIRCUIT COURSES

"Dream barriers look very high until someone climbs them. They are not barriers anymore." ▪ Lasse Viren

One could say that these ultra-distance races attract only an exclusive group of athletes and take place in only a handful of locations, which is unlike many other events where most of the time you can count on a drive within a certain distance of your home to participate. While the Ultra-Distance Triathlons are not the most popular sport, they do draw in an elite group of athletes willing to challenge themselves mentally to take on these courses.

If you are considering training for one of these races, first make sure you have all of the facts about the demands of each individual race. These races will command a significant level of endurance and stamina. You must be mentally and physically prepared to participate — all in and no holds barred. The extended distances alone require the utmost preparation to get to the finish line.

So, before you make any concrete decisions to add an Ultra-Distance Triathlon on your goal list, let's review some of the specific race distances and circuit courses. What should an athlete know about these distances? And what kind of courses will present what kind of challenges that you must prepare yourself to overcome?

The ultra-distance athlete must also have a total understanding of what kind of nutritional intake and training they can do ahead of time to prepare their bodies to tolerate abiding fatigue and discomfort and pain no one would ever experience in a shorter-distance race such as an Ironman Triathlon. Now any casual athletes reading this right now may wonder what is the appeal here? Well, it's the mental and physical challenge and ability to stay the literal course. If you've never experienced this level of being in the "zone" then it might be difficult to understand the drive, determination and passion that motivates athletes who compete at this level; but any ultra runner, ultra cyclist or adventure-racing athlete reading this will totally get it.

Know Your Race

We've already reviewed in the earlier chapter some of the races. Now it's time to get specific about each race and the distances involved. Some of you are going to review **Chart A** below and be a bit overwhelmed with the distances. Don't worry you can finish one of these races. For the endurance athlete who has only done a basic marathon or Ironman Triathlon, the distances may seem outrageous if not impossible; but I'm here to tell you that with the proper training and preparation, you can do it too. So, don't let **Chart A's** data make you close the book and forget your desire.

There are four major IUTA-certified Ultra-Distance Triathlon race distances that are as follows:

- Double
- Triple
- Quintuple
- Deca

Chart A – Race Distances

Race	Swim	Bike	Run
Double	7.6 km	360 km	84.4 km
Triple	11.4 km	540 km	126.6 km
Deca	38 km	1,800 km	422 km
Double Deca	76 km	3,600 km	844 km

I do need to mention the Double-Deca (20 Iron-man Distance events) and included it above. It was a race that took place in Monterrey, Mexico in 1998 — and was held for the second time in 2010. There were only four people in the world who finished a Double Deca Race in 1998. The four finishers of the Double Deca race in the Monterey, Mexico 1998 race were: Vidmantas Urbonas from Luanthia; Mardio Rodriguez from Mexico; Sylvia Andonie from Mexico; and Chet Blanton from the United States.

The "Ultraman" Races

There are also some other extreme triathlon races I have not mentioned here — the Ultraman series. I know it may seem like a stretch that you could have yet another race to challenge your "ultra"-endurance skills, but the Ultraman requires specific discipline applied over a three-day period. Participants are asked to race by invitation only for some races such as the Hawaii Ultraman, which limits the field size to 35. The Ultraman covers three days of demanding racing with a total of 515 kilometers and is a bit longer than the Double Ultra-Triathlon.

The Canadian Ultraman championship started in 1993, and this invitation-only race covers terrain in the Okanagan/Similkameen regions of British Columbia. This race is limited to 30 solo participants and features five relay teams made up of either two or three people.

While I want to mention these races, I do not intend to focus specific attention on them in this book. However, the training tools, plans and ideas are all applicable to the Ultraman races. I do think it's important for readers to be aware they exist as an alternative and uniquely different format to the four major races and categories mentioned above.

Circuit Courses

All of the major IUTA-certified races are held on closed-loop courses. The distances normally range from shorter one-mile loops for the running and biking disciplines. What's particularly interesting for the athlete is that the courses all have varying terrain. A few races include lake swims but the majority are pool swims. With the variances in the courses, athletes' strengths and weaknesses are challenged in different ways.

Circuit courses offer athletes more safety than an open course where random people and vehicles can cause potential collisions. Using a circuit course format allows the athlete to move from one discipline to the next with less concentration on unexpected distractions. Within this controlled environment, athletes are less likely to run into unexpected hazards that can cause injuries.

In the case of the Deca race held in Mexico, it requires over 900 loops on the bike alone. During this grueling 900-loop challenge, bikers become sleep deprived. As you fight to keep your eyes open, stay awake, and be on alert, the last thing you want to do is worry about oncoming traffic and cars that could cause a serious accident. Imagine the damage and chaos that would ensue from a group of sleep-deprived athletes running or riding their bikes on the open road.

The Ultraman series (held in Hawaii and Canada) offers the athlete open roads with specific assistance from crews who drive behind the athlete in a van or car. The IUTA races circuit format allow the crews to remain in one location to provide assistance and aid. Crew members are named "Super Crew" in Mexico. A crew is extremely important regardless of closed-circuit or open format.

The crew's participation also adds to what is a festive atmosphere where athletes and crew alike form bonds, friendships, and make connections with people from all over world. Many endurance races offer social activities before and after events, which give people time to bond and get to know each other.

When you have athletes who are already doing long distances including swimming, cycling and running, you do not need to create a course that is overly rugged and demanding with climbing-over mountains. These courses typically do not involve steep grades or require athletes to go up mountainsides or include mountain climbing at all nor are these courses as hilly as common triathlons. In fact, most of the races utilize flat or gently rolling terrain that, in and of itself, provides enough challenge for the athlete who already taxes his or her body over these long distances. The running and

TWITCH TIPS

There are two different types of Ultra-Distance Triathlons to consider — the Ultraman series (stage races held over three days) or the continuous format of the IUTA World Cup Series. Either race will offer plenty of challenges!

biking segments are usually done on asphalt roads and avoid dirt or single-track trails.

So I hope to have answered your big questions regarding the courses. If one of the things that was holding you back was the perception that not only do you have to swim, bike and run over hundreds of miles and cause further exertion on incredible and demanding courses, that is typically not the case. These races focus more on challenging the mind and body.

CHAPTER 3 – STEPPING UP TO THE DISTANCE

"Endurance is patience concentrated."
- Thomas Carlyle

As an athlete considering participation in Ultra-Distance Triathlons, you will be confronted with several questions key to your decision to not only get in the best physical shape to do the triathlon, but also understand what is involved and required of you physically and mentally. The first and foremost question I hear when I speak to athletes is: "Will the preparation require an enormous amount of training?" And before I go any further into that discussion, the answer is "yes;" but it is very manageable as you will see in future chapters.

Other notable and important questions include:

- I have a full-time job and/or family. How do I juggle all of the long workouts?

- What exactly is the weekly time commitment?
- Is the Double Triathlon race comparable in difficulty (both mentally and physically) to something such as a 100-mile mountain-trail race?
- Is it overly taxing to swim 4.8 miles or longer for these events?
- Where are the locations of the races?

So, let's walk you through and allow my guidance to help you answer these questions for yourself.

Preparation

As you saw in Chapter 2, the distances required for a Double Triathlon are double over the standard Ironman Race. Getting your body and mind in shape to confront these demands will, in fact, require a tremendous amount of time vested in proper training and preparation. You must consider many factors to step up your training for the distances demanded in these races, which will take you far beyond what you may have already done with an Ironman Triathlon.

In my opinion, the best way to start preparation is to participate in an Ironman Triathlon or ultra-running race, which will be a first incremental step toward being in a race for more than 12 hours at a time. You see 12 hours is just a fraction of the time it takes to do a Double Triathlon where the event may take over 24 hours.

By first confronting the preparatory demands of a 12-hour race, you mentally and physically put yourself on a training program that helps you stay the course on 24-hour-plus event. It will also give you real experience with what this is like on a small scale. If you're, say, a distance runner who believes that adding on the swimming and biking portions is not a big deal and you will start at this level, you will be unpleasantly surprised and set yourself up for failure. So know that even fast marathon runners or Ironman athletes must train differently for these events.

Getting Started

Since you're not going to jump right in and tackle an event of this size and length, I strongly recommend you begin by training for a 100-mile or 24-hour running race. And while I've witnessed athletes who have only completed ultra-running, ultra-cycling and adventure races do well in Ultra-Distance Triathlons — this is the exception not the rule. So, I don't want to mislead you if you have done some of these races that the same training will work for Ultra-Distance Triathlons.

Step 1: Make a plan. Like anything you intend to start and finish, I recommend you address questions about time and balancing your life with your training by creating a plan.

Step 2: Create goals. Your event plan should — like most strategic plans — address how much time you will set aside each day or week, establish incremental and doable goals (you don't want to set your sights too high from the start lest you disappoint yourself if you are unable to accomplish them), and outline these goals in a plan. It can be as simple as writing each goal on a single sheet of paper and then hanging it somewhere that you can readily review it. Somewhere you will frequently look at like a bulletin board or refrigerator — anything in your line of sight to keep you motivated and on task.

TWITCH TIPS

Start by writing down your dream, and then turn it into a goal with the addition of two items — add a deadline date to the dream and personalize it! For example, "I will complete a Double Ultra Triathlon by December 2011."

Example

Goal 1: Run daily every other morning

Goal 2: Bike long every weekend followed by a long run the next day

Goal 3: Swim a minimum of three times per week in the morning

Notice these goals are very simple. The specifics of distances and how to incrementally increase those goals will be addressed later in this book. These are just three general examples of what your plan should address. For now I just want you to get an idea of what I mean by designing your plan and setting up your goals. Notice that behind these goals is actually a routine. Routines help us develop habits. Getting into the habit of training nearly every day will help get you ready for these events.

Step 3: Making a training schedule. In the goals shown above, notice we mention mornings or evenings. You can create a specific schedule that enables you to train during the week, but my best advice to build up the necessary endurance is to save the longer distances for the weekends. If you have a family, you should carve out your family time and obligations and separate it from your training needs; but do be prepared to leave enough time to train for longer hours and miles. An idea that works well for many athletes is to train through the night during one weekend day. In Chapter 12, I will show you that you need not quit your job and divorce your wife or husband to prepare for these longer events. It's about just what I've said — schedules. Schedules help keep everything in life in balance.

Also, remember that you will be racing for sometimes over 24 hours, which inconveniently means you race at night as well as day. So, your schedule must address nighttime training and even press your fatigue and desire for sleep. Sleep deprivation can be an ultra-distance athlete's foe as noted in Chapter 2. So, it's imperative that you become comfortable with being out at night and fatigued enough to where you build your reflex muscle to stay awake and alert.

Let me give you a caveat: The first experience riding at night and feeling comfortable while sleep deprived will challenge you early on. You will get used to the routine, and soon it will become second nature. Not building your "night-time-alert" muscle up can be deadly. In Chapter 4, I will illustrate how you can simulate overnight training as well.

Step 4: Be prepared to train your mind. Significant training is done to prepare for the hard challenge late into the race — the run. You will need the proper "mindset" to deal with challenges such as fatigued legs that can cause the desire to buckle and give up during an Ultra-Distance Triathlon (I will address this more in Chapter 4). This is where your mental preparedness and training plays a key role in whether or not you cross that finish line.

You must be prepared to run with fatigued legs no matter what. I've seen many fast marathon runners slogging through these races with a tired shuffle where it's a challenge just to keep moving. Nothing will challenge you more than the leg fatigue except the mental factor. With the right mindset, no amount of fatigue will take you down. It is the right mental outlook that will carry you over that finish line — and like I've said, finishing in these races is everything. I'm going to teach you to overcome this kind of fatigue through focused "fatigue-run" training sessions that will benefit you late into your race.

Step 5: Apply strategies to overcome tired legs. Again, while I will delve deeper into this in Chapter 4, I do want you to introduce training plan-strategies designed to help you cope and overcome tired legs. Here are three such strategies you can apply:

- **Pick several triathlons or ultra-running races that are shorter in overall time and do not taper for the race.** The key is to build in long training sessions of running right up to the race. No, you won't be setting a run PR (personal record); but it will train the body and mind to learn how to run with fatigued legs.
- **Apply several three-day, high-mileage sessions back to back.** An example would be to include long sessions of biking and running for three straight days and have a very long run on the third day.
- **Incorporate a longer ultra-running race into the training program of 100K in length or longer.** This will prepare you to "go the distance" and give you experience and knowledge of training at this level to help you build proper endurance over extreme distances — and not make the actual race the first time you've ever done this kind of distance.

Step 6: Start learning to sit in the "saddle" for long distances. Maybe you've done a 112-mile bike ride as part of your Ironman distance training, but have you ever biked two or three times that distance? If not, you need to build up to it and confront tired legs, back pain, sore wrists, neck, saddle sores, etc. Stepping up your biking distances gives you the proper perspective and experience to understand what it's going to take in the actual event.

And let me ask you this: Can an individual who only includes 100-mile rides finish a Double Triathlon? Yes, but I have seen many individuals drop out during the bike discipline or first several miles of the run. Why? They did not spend adequate time training for the long bike section of the race. It's a big difference riding six hours versus 14 hours or more.

Consistent Training to Finish

You cannot expect to finish these Ultra-Distance Triathlons by applying an inconsistent training routine. You must prepare a plan, create a schedule, and apply it. Please be advised to make it manageable. Build up to the proper distances over time. Be reasonable to your body. Break down your plan (including mental training) in smaller increments where you build up to your goals over several months. Be kind to your body and mind — otherwise, you will be tempted to believe you can't do it. You can! And you will — with the right training program.

CHAPTER 4 – TRAINING PROGRAM – DOUBLE ULTRA TRIATHLON

"Excellence is an art won by training and habituation. We do not act rightly because we have virtue or excellence, but we rather have those because we have acted rightly. We are what we repeatedly do. Excellence, then, is not an act but a habit."

- Aristotle

Here we are. This is probably the chapter you immediately flipped to after looking at the table of contents — the training program chapter! Training plays an important role in just about anything we do whether in our careers, or in this case, an Ultra-Distance Triathlon. And like you, I was no different in my intrigue about actual training programs or specific workouts. As a lifetime learner, I continue to read various books on triathlons, marathons and ultra-distance events. I wanted to know and learn everything I can in order to properly prepare to reach my goal of crossing the finishing line. I knew that to achieve my dream, I would have to get ready. Now I'm going to pass onto you what I learned about training.

YEARS OF KISS

As I highlighted earlier, I receive many requests from athletes on how should they train to take the first major step up from the traditional Ironman Distance to the Double Ultra Triathlon. In this chapter, I will cover specific training cycles for 20 weeks to build up to the Double Ultra distance. The various other Ultra-Distance Triathlons (Triple and Quintuple) can easily be adapted to these models. So let's get started. If you are interested in Deca Training programs, please feel free to email me at wayne.kurtz@racetwitch.com.

For 25 years of endurance racing, I have believed in the KISS (Keep it Simple Stupid) Theory with a heavy focus on common sense. The workouts I have outlined each have a specific purpose — be it strength, muscular endurance, interval sets, or long mental training days — combined with a continuous mix of variety to keep everything fresh.

I want to reiterate that these programs will only work if you are consistent with the training. The hourly and weekly schedules can be adjusted, but my recommendation is that to be successful you will need to complete a minimum of 85 percent of the overall workouts each week. Yes there are exceptions, but I am referencing the vast majority of athletes who attempt to jump to these distances. These are baseline plans of what has worked for me and other athletes I have coached over the years. I've based these plans on years of experience as I continue to implement new training methods. It's not the only approach by any means that you must complete all these workouts and not add enhancements or changes to your own personal schedule. I am a huge fan of all of the great books by Matt Fitzgerald, who has produced and shared many of his philosophies regarding training, including his recent book *RUN: The Mind-Body Method of Running by Feel.*

There are going to be times that you might want to change up the schedule. For example, instead of another long weekend of training you might shorten the workouts while increasing the overall intensity. In many cases, you will need to go by your own "feel" and remember to use common sense. Many times I have seen athletes who tell me they had a bad race and were unhappy with the result, but I also remember them telling me that they had an epic training session. Remember, you want to have fun in your training but don't ever leave your race-day peak performance out on a training ride/run workout!

This training schedule for the Double Ultra is designed for experienced athletes. As I mentioned earlier, I strongly recommend you compete in any of the following races prior to the goal of the Ultra-Distance Triathlon, such as several different Ironman Distance events, ultra running or long-distance cycling races. These training schedules are focused and will be difficult and present challenges that you will face during the race. Be smart in your training and gradually progress over time. I have started these schedules, assuming you already have established many weeks of base-building mileage. These schedules are the key weeks of your training progression. The training schedules are built upon the theory of six-week cycles with the sixth week being an active recovery week along with Time-Trial Progression Workouts to be used for future tracking — this approach was introduced to me many years ago by my long-term friend and coach Nate Llerandi, who has been a tremendous personal resource over the years for me. The schedules incorporate his vast experience working with me to formulate specific training schedules for all of my Ultra-Distance Triathlons. Nate's theories on training mesh with mine, and we have built a great partnership over the years working together. Nate's expertise in assisting and building comprehensive training plans has been instrumental in my progression over the years no question!

Training Zones: To keep things basic the following are the various levels of training exertion: L1 means Level 1, L2 means Level 2, etc. Heart rate (HR) and the percentage ranges are based upon your lactic threshold. As experienced endurance athletes, you are probably familiar with the recommendation to use a heart-rate monitor. If you need a resource book, check out the classic Sally Edwards book, *Heart Rate Monitor Book* to highlight the specific zone targets.

L1: 55–70 percent Max HR
L2: 65–78 percent Max HR
L3: 76–86 percent Max HR
Sweet Spot: 75–88 percent Max HR
L4: 84–92 percent Max HR
L5: 90–96 percent Max HR
L6: 93–96 percent Max HR
L7: Max Effort; HR insignificant due to short nature of efforts

As you will notice, I base all the training schedules upon total time versus miles/kilometers. The highest volume weeks are in the 24-hour range with the majority of them around 20 hours per week. I have outlined a 20-week training schedule including a taper week prior to the race. Be advised, do not take these schedules lightly and jump from a normal eight-hour training week to over 20 hours, as you will see in week one. Be sensible and incorporate base-building weeks to get to these higher weekly training hours. If you jump too early, you're experienced enough to know that injuries can start occurring by not using common sense.

Time-Trial Progression Workouts and Tracking

You will notice a series of baseline time trials that will be monitored over the training cycles. These should be performed on week six and 12.

TEST (best done at the track)
(referenced in weekly training schedules)
RUN 1:15 (1 hour, 15 minutes)

- Warm up the first 15 minutes. Then complete 4-6x 20-second pick-ups (build the curves – cruise the straights). Then take a couple of minutes to get prepped for the test.

- TEST: Five-mile aerobic TT (time trial). Set your HR

monitor to beat three beats below and three beats above. Target 75 percent HR zone.

- 75 percent (creating an effective five-beat, non-beeping zone). Slow down or speed up accordingly when your HR monitor starts beeping. Get your mile splits as well as overall time to compare to future tests.
- Cool down the rest of the time at L1

TEST BIKE 2:00 – on the Indoor Trainer (referenced in weekly training schedules)

1. Warm up the first 15 minutes. Then complete 5x (1 minutes L4 at 100-110 rpm (revolutions per minute) with 1 minute L1). Then spin easy at L1 for 5 minutes before the first test.
2. TEST: 5 minutes at 80 percent of your last 5 minutes test – strong but controlled.
3. 20-25 minutes super easy spinning
4. 20 minutes all out, going for best average watts
5. Then spin at L2 until you have 15 minutes left. Shut it down and cool down at L1 the rest of the time.
6. Record distance, HR and average watts.

MULTIPLE CROSS-TRAINING STRENGTH TEST – 45 MINUTES (referenced in weekly training schedules)

1. 5-minutes warm up easy on the bike spinning
2. 10 minutes very hard resistance gear seated on the indoor trainer
3. Immediately jump off the bike and do 100 Hindu Squats (see page 116) with medium weight
4. After squats jump rope for 5 minutes straight
5. 10 minutes very hard resistance gear standing (2 minutes, seated 1 minute)
6. Immediately jump off bike and do 125 Hindu Squats (no weights)
7. 5 minutes of jumping rope
8. 50 pushups
9. The goal with this workout is to increase the number of reps and overall power output on the bike over time.

Strength Training – Workout for Training Schedules (referenced in weekly training schedules)

Two Super Sets

1. 8 squat jumps, working on maximum height. "Coil up" at a moderate speed, then explode up. Can

hold a dumbbell between legs.

2. 12 push-up to side plank. Controlled down, then explode the arms up and into a side plank (six to each side, alternating).

3. 60-second rest from first set to second set

Two Super Sets

- 12 single leg squats to a chair/bench, press up all the way to the toes and jump up, switching legs in mid-air.

- 20 fit-ball (large exercise ball) hamstring curls

- 60-second rest from first set to second set

Two Super Sets

- 20 single leg step-ups on a bench. Keep heel down and then press through to the toes at end of leg extension. Jump up, land on other foot, and repeat. Can use up to 40 lbs total weight.

- 12 back extensions on a fit ball. Position fit ball under abdomen/chest and raise the legs as high as you can. Mimic a dolphin swim.

- 60-second rest from first set to second set

Two Super Sets

- 50 thrust squats. Come down as far as your leg bends during pedaling motion; allow arms to raise in front of you as you squat then lower them back to your side as you stand up. As fast as you can do these, but controlled (not jerky).

- 60 bicycle kicks – 30 to each side. Again, fast cadence as you switch one elbow/knee to the other but controlled (not jerky).
- 60-second rest from first set to second set

Two Super Sets

- 100 Hindu Squats at a fast tempo, but in control with good form
- Plank (page 116) – total time 1:30
- 60-second rest from first set to second set

Training Plan for Double Ultra Triathlon

Please note: This is a training plan designed for a Double Ultra Triathlon and the training needs of this event.

Please note all swim workouts are listed in meters: For example: 12 x 25 with :10 means 12, 25 meter sprints with 10-second rest between each one.

☑ TRAINING PLAN FOR DOUBLE ULTRA TRIATHLON

WEEK 1

TOTAL HOURS: 20:30

Training Zones
L1: 55–70 percent Max HR
L2: 65–78 percent Max HR
L3: 76–86 percent Max HR
Sweet Spot: 75–88 percent Max HR
L4: 84–92 percent Max HR
L5: 90–96 percent Max HR
L6: 93–96 percent Max HR
L7: Max Effort; HR insignificant due to short nature of efforts

❶ Monday

SWIM 0:45 easy L1; your choice, but make sure you include at least 500 meters kicking

BIKE 0:45

- Aerobic recovery at L1

STRENGTH TRAINING WORKOUT (see workout, page 38)

❷ Tuesday

BIKE 2:00

- Warm up the first 20 minutes. Then complete 5x (30 second L4 with 30 second L1). Do these spin-ups at 100 + rpm to get the legs ready for the main set. Then spin easy for 5 minutes before the main set.

- Main set: 4 x 8 minutes L4 with 4 minutes easy L1. If you can, do these up a climb and descend back down for recovery. Use the first rep as the benchmark for the others.
- Cool down the rest of the time at L1/L2, steady aerobic

RUN 1:15

- Warm up the first 10 minutes. Then hold your HR at L2 for the middle 55 minutes. For the final: 15 of every 5:00, surge to L5 (3K-5K race effort), then settle back into your aerobic pace. This is to help with leg turnover speed and lengthening your stride.
- Cool down the rest of the time at L1

❸ Wednesday

RUN 1:00 – Hill Repeats/Functional Training with Hindu Squats

- Warm up the first 15 minutes. Then complete 6x 20-second pick-ups (build straights – cruise curves). Then jog easy for a couple minutes before the main set.
- Main set: 5-6 total hill repeats (can be trails or roads) – strong and steady, recover with easy run to the bottom. Climb under control. For

hill repeat numbers 2 and 4 when you get to the bottom after recovery, perform 100 Hindu Squats.

- Cool down the rest of the time, gradually below 65 percent

BIKE 0:30

- Aerobic recovery at L1

❹ Thursday

SWIM 0:45

- 1,800-2,000 meters straight at L1
- Get into a rhythm and hold steady the whole time

BIKE 1:30

- L1/L2 ride; easy pressure on the pedals. Keep HR below 70 percent, which dictates where your power should be (if on the indoor bike trainer).

STRENGTH-TRAINING WORKOUT (see workout, page 38)

❺ Friday

SWIM 1:15

- 400 S (swim) – 200 K (kick) – 200 P (pull) warm up, continuous
- 12 x 25 with: 10; alternate build up – build down – easy – fast
- 2 x 100 easy with: 15
- 4-6 sets of: 200 L2 with: 30

- 100 L3 with: 20
- 50 L4 with: 10
- 50 L1 with: 10
- 1,000 Pull at 70 percent; steady pace and effort
- 500 kick L1
- 300 swim L1

RUN 0:45

- Easy recovery at L1

❻ <u>Saturday</u>

BIKE 6:00 – group ride OK

- Dynamic ride, mainly L1/L2, but allow time to press up and over any short rolling hills, etc. In the final 2 hrs, complete 3 x 20 minutes L3 with 10 minutes L1 between. Strong, steady and relaxed as you fatigue. The most important aspects of the ride are the time in the saddle and pushing the pace when the legs are tired later into the ride.
- Cool down the rest of the time L1

RUN 0:45 – right after biking

- L2 for the first 30 minutes. Settle into a steady pace/effort. Then cool down the rest of the time at L1.

❼ <u>Sunday</u>

RUN 3:00 (trails or roads)

- Warm up the first 15 minutes. Then hold your HR at L1-2 for the middle 2:30. Negative split your effort over a rolling course. Punch it up and over 10 of the shorter hills – efforts of around 30-45 seconds – with varying amounts of settling back into L1-2 between these punctuated efforts.
- Cool down the rest of the time at L1

☑ TRAINING PLAN FOR DOUBLE ULTRA TRIATHLON
WEEK 2
TOTAL HOURS: 21:15

Training Zones
L1: 55–70 percent Max HR
L2: 65–78 percent Max HR
L3: 76–86 percent Max HR
Sweet Spot: 75–88 percent Max HR
L4: 84–92 percent Max HR
L5: 90–96 percent Max HR
L6: 93–96 percent Max HR
L7: Max Effort; HR insignificant due to short nature of efforts

➊ Monday
SWIM 0:45 complete L1 recovery; your choice
BIKE 0:45

- Aerobic recovery at L1

➋ Tuesday
BIKE 2:00

- Warm up the first 20 minutes. Then complete 5x (30 seconds L4 with 30 seconds L1). Do these spin-ups at 100 + rpm to get the legs ready for the main set. Then spin easy for 5 minutes before the main set.

- Main set: 3 x 10 minutes hard – 6-7 minutes easy L1. Each 10 minutes rep done as: 3 minutes L5 – 1 minute L4 – 2 minutes L5 – 1 minute L4 – 1 minute L5 – 1 minutes L4 – 2 x 20 second L6 with 10 second L1 between. For the L5, shoot for at least 110 percent; for L4, shoot for below 95 percent.
- Cool down the rest of the time at L1

RUN 1:15

- Warm up the first 10 minutes. Then hold your HR at L2 for the middle 55 minutes. For the final: 15 of every 5:00, surge to L5 (3K–5K race effort), then settle back into your aerobic pace. This is to help with leg turnover speed and lengthening your stride.
- Cool down the rest of the time at L1

❸ <u>Wednesday</u>

RUN 1:00 – Hill Repeats/Functional Training with Hindu Squats

- Warm up the first 15 minutes. Then complete 6x 20-second pick-ups (build straights – cruise curves). Then jog easy for a couple minutes before the main set.
- Main set: 5-6 hill repeats (can be trails or roads) – strong and steady, recover with easy run to the bottom. Climb under control. For

hill repeat numbers 2 and 4 when you get to the bottom after recovery, perform 100 Hindu Squats.

- Cool down the rest of the time, gradually below 65 percent.

BIKE 0:30

- Aerobic recovery at L1

❹ **Thursday**

SWIM 1:30

- 400 S – 200 K – 200 P warm up, continuous
- 12 x 25 with: 10; alternate build up – build down – easy – fast
- 2 x 100 easy with: 15
- 12 x 200 with: 30 (2 at 70-78 percent – 1 at 50-60 percent)
- 500 pull at 70 percent cool down; steady pace and effort
- 12 x 50 at L3 with: 15; strong and steady
- 8-10 x 50 with: 10, cool down

BIKE 1:30

- L1/L2 ride; easy pressure on the pedals. Keep HR below 70 percent, which dictates where your power should be (if on the indoor bike trainer).

STRENGTH-TRAINING WORKOUT (see workout, page 38)

❺ <u>Friday</u>

SWIM 0:30

- 15-21 x 100 continuous, alt 100 S-K-P

RUN 0:45

- Easy recovery at L1.

❻ **<u>Saturday</u> – brick – if possible do the workout through the night (ride with bike lights outside)**

BIKE 4:00

- Steady L1/L2 effort

RUN 2:00

- Get changed and out the door as soon as possible. Settle in at L1/L2. Negative split the run, finishing strong but controlled.
- Allow enough time for adequate cool down

❼ <u>Sunday</u>

BIKE 4:00

- Steady L1/L2 effort – more important to put in the time than to press the effort. If you find yourself "driving" the effort, pull back just a little bit and keep things light.

☑ TRAINING PLAN FOR DOUBLE ULTRA TRIATHLON
WEEK 3
TOTAL HOURS: 20:30

Training Zones
L1: 55–70 percent Max HR
L2: 65–78 percent Max HR
L3: 76–86 percent Max HR
Sweet Spot: 75–88 percent Max HR
L4: 84–92 percent Max HR
L5: 90–96 percent Max HR
L6: 93–96 percent Max HR
L7: Max Effort; HR insignificant due to short nature of efforts

❶ Monday
SWIM 1:00 easy L1; your choice

❷ Tuesday
BIKE 2:00

- Warm up the first 20 minutes. Then complete 5x (30 seconds L4 with 30 seconds L1). Do these spin-ups at 100 + rpm to get the legs ready for the main set. Then spin easy for 5 minutes before the main set.
- Main set: 3 x 12 minutes L4 with 6 minutes easy

L1. If you can, do these up a climb and descend back down for recovery. Use the first rep as the benchmark for the others.

- Cool down the rest of the time at L1/L2, steady aerobic

RUN 1:15

- Warm up the first 10 minutes. Then hold your HR at L2 for the middle 55 minutes. For the final: 15 of every 5:00, surge to L5 (3K-5K race effort), then settle back into your aerobic pace. This is to help with leg turnover speed and lengthening your stride.
- Cool down the rest of the time at L1

❸ Wednesday

RUN 1:15 – at the track

- Warm up the first 15 minutes. Then complete 6x (build straights – cruise curves). Then jog easy for a couple minutes before the main set.
- Main set: 2 sets of 5x (1,000 L3 with 200 L1); extra 800 easy between sets – strong and steady.
- Cool down the rest of the time, gradually below 65 percent.

BIKE 0:30

- Aerobic recovery at L1

❹ Thursday

SWIM 0:45

- 1,800-2,000 straight swim at L1. Get into a rhythm and hold steady the whole time.

BIKE 1:30

- L1/L2 ride; easy pressure on the pedals. Keep HR below 70 percent, which dictates where your power should be (if on the indoor bike trainer).

STRENGTH-TRAINING WORKOUT (see workout, page 38)

❺ Friday

SWIM 1:30

- 400 S – 200 K – 200 P warm up, continuous
- 12 x 25 with: 10; alternate build up – build down – easy – fast
- 2 x 100 easy with: 15
- 3 sets of: 500 L2 with 1:00
- 8 x 50 L3 with: 15
- 100 easy with: 15
- 1,000 Pull at 70 percent; steady pace and effort
- 500 Kick L1
- 300 Swim L1

RUN 0:45

- Easy recovery at L1

❻ <u>Saturday</u>

BIKE 6:00 – group ride

- Dynamic ride, mainly L1/L2, but allow time to press up and over any short rolling hills, etc. In the final two hours, complete 2 x 30 minutes L3 with 10-15 minutes L1 between. Strong, steady and relaxed as you fatigue.
- Cool down the rest of the time L1

❼ <u>Sunday</u>

RUN 4:00

- Warm up the first 15 minutes. Then hold your HR at L1-2 for the middle 3:30. Negative split your effort over a rolling course. Punch it up and over 10 of the shorter hills – efforts of around 30-45 second – with varying amounts of settling back into L1-2 between these punctuated efforts.
- Cool down the rest of the time at L1

☑ TRAINING PLAN FOR DOUBLE ULTRA TRIATHLON
WEEK 4
TOTAL HOURS: 23:00

Training Zones
L1: 55–70 percent Max HR
L2: 65–78 percent Max HR
L3: 76–86 percent Max HR
Sweet Spot: 75–88 percent Max HR
L4: 84–92 percent Max HR
L5: 90–96 percent Max HR
L6: 93–96 percent Max HR
L7: Max Effort; HR insignificant due to short nature of efforts

❶ **Monday**

SWIM 0:45 complete L1 recovery – your choice
BIKE 0:45
- Aerobic recovery at L1

STRENGTH-TRAINING WORKOUT (see workout, page 38)

❷ **Tuesday**

BIKE 2:00
- Warm up the first 20 minutes. Then complete 5x (30 seconds L4 with 30 seconds L1). Do these spin-ups at 100 + rpm to get the legs ready for

the main set. Then spin easy for 5 minutes before the main set.

- Main set: 3 x 10 minutes hard – 5-6 minutes easy L1. Each 10 minutes rep done as: 3 minutes L5; 1 minute L4; 2 minutes L5; 1 minute L4; 1 minute L5; 1 minute L4 – 2 x 20 second L6 with 10 seconds L1 between. For the L5, shoot for at least 110 percent; for L4, shoot for below 95 percent.
- Cool down the rest of the time at L1

RUN 1:15

- Warm up the first 10 minutes. Then hold your HR at L2 for the middle 55 minutes. For the final: 15 of every 5:00, surge to L5 (3K-5K race effort), then settle back into your aerobic pace. This is to help with leg turnover speed and lengthening your stride.
- Cool down the rest of the time at L1

❸ <u>Wednesday</u>

RUN 1:15 – at the track

- Warm up the first 15 minutes. Then complete 6x 20-second pick-ups (build straights – cruise curves). Then jog easy for a couple minutes before the main set.
- Main set: 2 sets of 3x (1,600 L3 with 400 easy jog); extra 800 easy between sets.
- Cool down the rest of the time, gradually below 65 percent.

BIKE 1:00

- Aerobic recovery at L1

❹ Thursday

SWIM 1:30

- 400 S – 200 K – 200 P warm up, continuous
- 12 x 25 with: 10; alternate build up – build down – easy – fast
- 2 x 100 easy with: 15
- 40 x 50 with: 10. Odds L2; evens L3
- 500 pull at 70 percent cool down; steady pace and effort
- 3 x 200 kick L2 with: 30
- 8-10 x 50 with: 10, cool down

BIKE 1:30

- L1/L2 ride; easy pressure on the pedals. Keep HR below 70 percent, which dictates where your power should be (if on the indoor bike trainer).

STRENGTH-TRAINING WORKOUT (see workout, page 38)

❺ Friday

SWIM 0:30

- 15-21 x 100 continuous, alt 100 S-K-P

RUN 1:00

- Easy recovery at L1

❻ Saturday

BIKE 6:00 – group ride OK

- Dynamic ride, mainly L1/L2, but allow time to press up and over any short rolling hills, etc. In the final two-plus hours, complete 3 x 25 minutes L3 with 10 minutes L1 between. Strong, steady and relaxed as you fatigue.
- Cool down the rest of the time L1

❼ Sunday

RUN 1:00

- First thing in the morning. L1/L2 effort, steady and controlled.

BIKE 4:00 – either right after running or soon after

- Steady L1/L2 effort – more important to put in the time than to press the effort. If you find yourself "driving" the effort, pull back just a little bit and keep things light.

☑ TRAINING PLAN FOR DOUBLE ULTRA TRIATHLON
WEEK 5
TOTAL HOURS: 21:00

Training Zones
L1: 55–70 percent Max HR
L2: 65–78 percent Max HR
L3: 76–86 percent Max HR
Sweet Spot: 75–88 percent Max HR
L4: 84–92 percent Max HR
L5: 90–96 percent Max HR
L6: 93–96 percent Max HR
L7: Max Effort; HR insignificant due to short nature of efforts

❶ Monday
SWIM 1:00 easy L1; your choice
STRENGTH-TRAINING WORKOUT (see workout, page 38)

❷ Tuesday
BIKE 2:00

- Warm up the first 20 minutes. Then complete 5x (30 second L4 with 30 second L1). Do these spin-ups at 100 + rpm to get the legs ready for the main set. Then spin easy for 5 minutes before the main set.

- Main set: 3 x 15 minutes L4 with 7 minutes easy L1. If you can, do these up a climb and descend back down for recovery. Use the first rep as the benchmark for the others.
- Cool down the rest of the time at L1/L2, steady aerobic

RUN 1:15

- Warm up the first 10 minutes. Then hold your HR at L2 for the middle 55 minutes. For the final: 15 of every 5:00, surge to L5 (3K-5K race effort), then settle back into your aerobic pace. This is to help with leg turnover speed and lengthening your stride.
- Cool down the rest of the time at L1

❸ <u>Wednesday</u>

RUN 1:15 – at the track

- Warm up the first 15 minutes. Then complete 6x 20-second pick-ups (build straights – cruise curves). Then jog easy for a couple minutes before the main set.
- Main set: 40 minutes L3; see how much ground you can cover!
- Cool down the rest of the time, gradually below 65 percent.

BIKE 0:30

- Aerobic recovery at L1

❹ <u>Thursday</u>

SWIM 0:45

- 1,800-2,000 straight at L1. Get into a rhythm and hold steady the whole time.

BIKE 1:30

- L1/L2 ride; easy pressure on the pedals. Keep HR below 70 percent, which dictates where your power should be (if on the indoor bike trainer).

STRENGTH-TRAINING WORKOUT (see workout, page 38)

❺ <u>Friday</u>

SWIM 1:30

- 400 S – 200 K – 200 P warm up, continuous
- 12 x 25 with: 10; alternate build up – build down – easy – fast
- 2 x 100 easy with: 15
- 5 x 500 L2 with 1:00; can pull even repeats. Steady, sustainable effort here.
- 1,000 Pull at 70 percent; steady pace and effort
- 8-12 x 50 with: 10 cool down

RUN 0:30

- Easy recovery at L1

❻ <u>Saturday</u> – brick; look for improvement over this workout last cycle. I would recommend if possible to do this workout throughout the night

BIKE 3:00

- L1/L2. Putting in the time. Focus on "going the distance" today.

RUN 1:30

- L1/L2. Putting in the time. Focus on "going the distance" today.

BIKE 2:00

- L1/L2. Putting in the time. Focus on "going the distance" today.

RUN 1:00

- L1/L2. Putting in the time. Focus on "going the distance" today.

❼ Sunday

RUN 3:00

- Steady L1/L2 effort. Just get used to slogging through it when the legs are heavy and fatigued from yesterday.

☑ TRAINING PLAN FOR DOUBLE ULTRA TRIATHLON

WEEK 6

TOTAL HOURS: 11:00

Training Zones
L1: 55–70 percent Max HR
L2: 65–78 percent Max HR
L3: 76–86 percent Max HR
Sweet Spot: 75–88 percent Max HR
L4: 84–92 percent Max HR
L5: 90–96 percent Max HR
L6: 93–96 percent Max HR
L7: Max Effort; HR insignificant due to short nature of efforts

❶ **Monday – DAY OFF**

❷ **Tuesday**

SWIM 0:30

- 6 x 100, alt S-K-P continuous
- 16-20 x 50 L1 with: 10 (3 swim – 1 kick)

BIKE 0:45

- Aerobic recovery at L1

STRENGTH-TRAINING WORKOUT (see workout, page 38)

❸ Wednesday
RUN 1:00

- Complete L1 recovery effort

❹ Thursday
BIKE 1:00

- Aerobic recovery at L1

❺ Friday – **TEST (best done at the track)**
RUN 1:15

- Warm up the first 15 minutes. Then complete 4-6x 20-second pick-ups (build the curves – cruise the straights). Then take a couple minutes to get prepped for the test.
- TEST: 5-mile aerobic TT. Set your HR monitor to beat three beats below and three beats above 75 percent (creating an effective five-beat, non-beeping zone). Slow down or speed up accordingly when your HR monitor starts beeping. Get your mile splits as well as overall time to compare to future tests.
- Cool down the rest of the time at L1

SWIM 0:45

- 200 S-K-P Continuous
- 5 x 100 L2 with: 20
- 2 x 50 easy with: 10
- 600 pull at upper L1
- 4-8 x 50 with: 10 cool down, your choice

❻ Saturday

BIKE 2:00 – on the Indoor Bike Trainer

- Warm up the first 15 minutes. Then complete 5x (1 minutes L4 at 100-110 rpm with 1 minute L1). Then spin easy at L1 for 5 minutes before the first test.
- TEST: 5 minutes at 80 percent of your last 5 minutes test – strong but controlled.
- 20-25 minutes super easy spinning
- 20 minutes all out, going for best average watts
- Then spin at L2 until you have 15 minutes left. Shut it down and cool down at L1 the rest of the time.

SWIM 0:45

- 600 pull at upper L1
- 5x (100 kick –: 15 – 150 swim — : 20). Kicks are upper L2; swims are descend 1-5 from low L1 to upper L2.
- 6-10 x 50 with: 10 cool down

❼ Sunday

RUN 3:00

- Warm up the first 15 minutes. Then hold your HR at L1-2 for the middle 2:30. Negative split your effort over a rolling course. Punch it up and over 10 of the shorter hills — efforts of around 30-45 second — with varying amounts of settling back into L1-2 between these punctuated efforts.
- Cool down the rest of the time at L1

STRENGTH-TRAINING WORKOUT (see workout, page 38)

☑ TRAINING PLAN FOR DOUBLE ULTRA TRIATHLON

WEEK 7

TOTAL HOURS: 24:45

Training Zones

L1: 55–70 percent Max HR

L2: 65–78 percent Max HR

L3: 76–86 percent Max HR

Sweet Spot: 75–88 percent Max HR

L4: 84–92 percent Max HR

L5: 90–96 percent Max HR

L6: 93–96 percent Max HR

L7: Max Effort; HR insignificant due to short nature of efforts

❶ Monday

SWIM 0:45 easy L1; your choice

BIKE 0:45

- Aerobic recovery at L1

STRENGTH-TRAINING WORKOUT (see workout, page 38) **(include at least 200 Hindu Squats in the workout)**

❷ Tuesday

BIKE 2:00

- Warm up the first 20 minutes
- Main set: 2 x 20 minutes L3 with 10 minutes upper

L1 between; strong aerobic to tempo effort, working on getting in a groove more than forcing the pace/ effort. After the second recovery period, settle into steady L2 effort until it's time to cool down.

- Cool down the rest of the time at L1

RUN 1:15

- Warm up the first 10 minutes. Then hold your HR at L2 for the middle 55 minutes. For the final: 15 of every 5:00, surge to L5 (3K-5K race effort), then settle back into your aerobic pace. This is to help with leg turnover speed and lengthening your stride.
- Cool down the rest of the time at L1

❸ Wednesday

RUN 1:15

- Warm up the first 20 minutes
- Main set: 2 x 15 minutes L3 with 8 minutes upper L1 between. Over rolling hills; strong and steady.
- Cool down the rest of the time at L1

BIKE/ Jump Rope 0:30

- Aerobic recovery at L1 on the bike then jump rope (on a cushioned surface or mat) for 3 minutes.

❹ Thursday

SWIM 1:30

- 400 S – 200 K – 200 P warm up, continuous
- 12 x 25 with: 10; alternate build up – build down

– easy – fast

- 2 x 100 easy with: 15
- 2 sets of: 1,000 pull at 70 percent; steady pace and effort; 30-second rest
- 12 x 50 with: 10, cycle through L1/L2/L3; 30 second rest after #12
- 500 Kick L1
- 500 Swim L1

BIKE 1:00

- L1/L2 ride; easy pressure on the pedals. Keep HR below 70 percent, which dictates where your power should be (if on the indoor bike trainer).

STRENGTH-TRAINING WORKOUT (see workout, page 38)

❺ <u>**Friday**</u>

RUN 3:00

- Warm up the first 15 minutes. Then hold your HR at L1/L2 for the middle 2:30. Negative split your effort over a rolling course. Punch it up and over 10 of the shorter hills – efforts of around 30-45 second – with varying amounts of settling back into L1-2 between these punctuated efforts.
- Cool down the rest of the time at L1

SWIM 0:45

- 1,800-2,000 Straight at L1. Get into a rhythm and hold steady the whole time.

❻ <u>Saturday</u>

BIKE 8:00 – group ride

- Dynamic ride, mainly L1/L2, but allow time to press up and over any short rolling hills, etc. In the final two hours, complete 3 x 20 minutes L3 with 10 minutes L1 between. Strong, steady and relaxed as you fatigue.
- Cool down the rest of the time L1

❼ <u>Sunday</u>

BIKE 4:00 – group ride – then jump rope

- Mainly L1, some L2 – all aerobic over a mostly flat course. Just put in the time here. After completing the ride do four sets of 1 minute of jump roping.

☑ TRAINING PLAN FOR DOUBLE ULTRA TRIATHLON WEEK 8

TOTAL HOURS: 21:45

Training Zones
L1: 55–70 percent Max HR
L2: 65–78 percent Max HR
L3: 76–86 percent Max HR
Sweet Spot: 75–88 percent Max HR
L4: 84–92 percent Max HR
L5: 90–96 percent Max HR
L6: 93–96 percent Max HR
L7: Max Effort; HR insignificant due to short nature of efforts

❶ Monday

SWIM 0:45 complete L1 recovery; your choice

RUN 0:45

- Aerobic recovery at L1

STRENGTH-TRAINING WORKOUT (see workout, page 38) **– include 3-5 minutes of jump rope**

❷ Tuesday

RUN 1:15

- Aerobic recovery at L1

SWIM 0:45 complete L1 recovery; your choice

❸ Wednesday

BIKE 2:00

- Warm up the first 20 minutes.
- Main set: 2 x 20 minutes L3 with 10 minutes upper L1 between, then an additional 10 minutes L3; strong aerobic to Tempo effort, working on getting in a groove more than forcing the pace/effort. After the 10 minutes L3, settle into steady L2 effort until it's time to cool down.
- Cool down the rest of the time at L1

RUN 1:15

- Warm up the first 10 minutes. Then hold your HR at L2 for the middle 55 minutes. For the final: 15 of every 5:00, surge to L5 (3K-5K race effort), then settle back into your aerobic pace. This is to help with leg turnover speed and lengthening your stride.
- Cool down the rest of the time at L1

❹ Thursday

SWIM 1:30

- 400 S – 200 K – 200 P warm up, continuous
- 12 x 25 with: 10; alternate build up – build down – easy – fast
- 2 x 100 easy with: 15
- 8 x 200 with: 30 (2 at 70-78 percent – 1 at 65-70 percent – 1 at 50-60 percent); right into

- 10 x 100 with: 20 (3 at 70-78 percent – 2 at 65-70 percent); right into
- 12 x 50 with: 10 (3 at 70-78 percent – 1 at 60-70 percent)
- 5-8 x 100 with: 15 (25 k-s-k-s), cool down

RUN 1:15

- Warm up the first 20 minutes
- Main set: 2 x 15 minutes L3 with 8 minutes upper L1 between, followed by another 8 minutes L3. Over rolling hills; strong and steady.
- Cool down the rest of the time at L1

❺ Friday

BIKE 1:30

- L1/L2 ride; easy pressure on the pedals. Keep HR below 70 percent, which dictates where your power should be (if on the indoor bike trainer).

RUN 0:45

- Easy recovery at L1

STRENGTH-TRAINING WORKOUT (see workout, page 38) **– Hindu Squats goal 250!**

❻ Saturday – brick

BIKE 4:00

- Steady L1/L2 effort

RUN 2:00

- Get changed and out the door ASAP. Settle in

at L1/L2. Negative split the run, finishing strong but controlled.
- Allow enough time for adequate cool down

❼ <u>Sunday</u>

BIKE 4:00

- Steady L1/L2 effort – more important to put in the time than to press the effort. If you find yourself "driving" the effort, pull back just a little bit and keep things light.

☑ TRAINING PLAN FOR DOUBLE ULTRA TRIATHLON
WEEK 9
TOTAL HOURS: 20:15

Training Zones
L1: 55–70 percent Max HR
L2: 65–78 percent Max HR
L3: 76–86 percent Max HR
Sweet Spot: 75–88 percent Max HR
L4: 84–92 percent Max HR
L5: 90–96 percent Max HR
L6: 93–96 percent Max HR
L7: Max Effort; HR insignificant due to short nature of efforts

❶ Monday
SWIM 1:00 easy L1; your choice
STRENGTH-TRAINING WORKOUT (see workout, page 38) **– include 4 sets of 1 minute jump rope**

❷ Tuesday
BIKE 2:00
- Warm up the first 20 minutes
- Main set: 3 x 20 minutes L3 with 10 minutes upper L1 between. Strong aerobic to Tempo effort, working on getting in a groove more than forcing

the pace/effort.
- Cool down the rest of the time at L1/L2

RUN 1:15
- Warm up the first 10 minutes. Then hold your HR at L2 for the middle 55 minutes. For the final: 15 of every 5:00, surge to L5 (3K-5K race effort), then settle back into your aerobic pace. This is to help with leg turnover speed and lengthening your stride.
- Cool down the rest of the time at L1

❸ Wednesday

RUN 1:15
- Warm up the first 20 minutes
- Main set: 3 x 15 minutes L3 with 8 minutes upper L1 between. Over rolling hills; strong and steady.
- Cool down the rest of the time at L1

BIKE 0:30
- Aerobic recovery at L1 – include 3 minutes of Jump rope after biking.

❹ Thursday

SWIM 1:00
- 3,000-4,000 straight at L1. Get into a rhythm and hold steady the whole time.

BIKE 1:00
- Aerobic recovery at L1

STRENGTH-TRAINING WORKOUT (see workout, page 38) **– include 300 Hindu Squats**

❺ <u>Friday</u>

SWIM 1:45

- 400 S – 200 K – 200 P warm up, continuous
- 12 x 25 with: 10; alternate build up – build down – easy – fast
- 2 x 100 easy with: 15
- 2 sets of: 600 L1 with 1:00
- 6 x 100 L2 with: 15
- 4 x 50 easy with: 15
- 1,000 pull at 70 percent; steady pace and effort
- 500 Kick L1
- 300 Swim L1

RUN 0:45

- Easy recovery at L1

❻ <u>Saturday</u>

BIKE 6:00 – group ride OK

- Dynamic ride, mainly L1/L2, but allow time to press up and over any short rolling hills, etc. In the final 90 minutes, complete 3 x 10 minutes L3 with 10 minutes L1 between. Strong, steady and relaxed as you fatigue.
- Cool down the rest of the time L1

❼ Sunday

RUN 4:00

- Warm up the first 15 minutes. Then hold your HR at L1-2 for the middle 3:30. Negative split your effort over a rolling course. Punch it up and over 10 of the shorter hills – efforts of around 30-45 second – with varying amounts of settling back into L1-2 between these punctuated efforts.
- Cool down the rest of the time at L1

☑ TRAINING PLAN FOR DOUBLE ULTRA TRIATHLON
WEEK 10
TOTAL HOURS: 23:00

Training Zones
L1: 55–70 percent Max HR
L2: 65–78 percent Max HR
L3: 76–86 percent Max HR
Sweet Spot: 75–88 percent Max HR
L4: 84–92 percent Max HR
L5: 90–96 percent Max HR
L6: 93–96 percent Max HR
L7: Max Effort; HR insignificant due to short nature of efforts

❶ <u>Monday</u>
SWIM 0:45 complete L1 recovery; your choice
BIKE 0:45
- Aerobic recovery at L1

STRENGTH-TRAINING WORKOUT (see workout, page 38)

❷ <u>Tuesday</u>
BIKE 2:00
- Warm up the first 20 minutes
- Main set: 2 x 30 minutes L3 with 15 minutes upper L1 between; strong aerobic to Tempo effort, working on getting in a groove more than forcing

the pace/effort.

- Cool down the rest of the time at L1/L2

RUN 1:15

- Warm up the first 10 minutes. Then hold your HR at L2 for the middle 55 minutes. For the final: 15 of every 5:00, surge to L5 (3K-5K race effort), then settle back into your aerobic pace. This is to help with leg turnover speed and lengthening your stride.
- Cool down the rest of the time at L1

❸ Wednesday

RUN 2:00

- L1/L2 effort. Relaxed, just put in the time.

BIKE 0:30

- L1 recovery, soon after running

❹ Thursday

SWIM 1:45

- 400 S – 200 K – 200 P warm up, continuous
- 12 x 25 with: 10; alternate build up – build down – easy – fast
- 2 x 100 easy with: 15
- 40 x 50 with: 10. Odds L2; evens L3
- 1,000 pull at 70 percent cool down; steady pace and effort
- 4 x 200 Kick L2 with: 30
- 12 x 50 with: 10, cool down

BIKE 1:30

- L1/L2 ride; easy pressure on the pedals. Keep HR below 70 percent, which dictates where your power should be (if on the indoor bike trainer).

STRENGTH-TRAINING WORKOUT (see workout, page 38)

❺ Friday

SWIM 0:30

- 15-21 x 100 continuous, alt 100 S-K-P

RUN 1:00

- Easy recovery at L1

❻ Saturday

BIKE 6:00 – group ride OK

- Steady L1/L2 effort – more important to put in the time than to press the effort. If you find yourself "driving" the effort, pull back just a little bit and keep things light.

❼ Sunday

RUN 1:00

- First thing in the morning. L1/L2 effort, steady and controlled.

BIKE 4:00 – either right after running or soon after

- Steady L1/L2 effort – more important to put in the time than to press the effort. If you find yourself "driving" the effort, pull back just a little bit and keep things light.

☑ TRAINING PLAN FOR DOUBLE ULTRA TRIATHLON
WEEK 11
TOTAL HOURS: 22:00

Training Zones
L1: 55–70 percent Max HR
L2: 65–78 percent Max HR
L3: 76–86 percent Max HR
Sweet Spot: 75–88 percent Max HR
L4: 84–92 percent Max HR
L5: 90–96 percent Max HR
L6: 93–96 percent Max HR
L7: Max Effort; HR insignificant due to short nature of efforts

❶ Monday
SWIM 1:00 easy L1; your choice
STRENGTH-TRAINING WORKOUT (see workout, page 38)
(include 4 minutes of jump rope)

❷ Tuesday
BIKE 2:00
- Warm up the first 30 minutes
- Main set: 60 minutes L3. Strong aerobic to tempo effort, working on getting in a groove more than forcing the pace/effort.

- Cool down the rest of the time at L1/L2

RUN 1:15

- Warm up the first 10 minutes. Then hold your HR at L2 for the middle 55 minutes. For the final: 15 of every 5:00, surge to L5 (3K-5K race effort), then settle back into your aerobic pace. This is to help with leg turnover speed and lengthening your stride.
- Cool down the rest of the time at L1

❸ Wednesday

RUN Trails 2:00

- L1/L2 effort. Relaxed, just put in the time.

BIKE 0:30

- L1 recovery, soon after running.

❹ Thursday

SWIM 0:45

- 1,800-2,000 straight at L1. Get into a rhythm and hold steady the whole time.

BIKE 1:30

- L1/L2 ride; easy pressure on the pedals. Keep HR below 70 percent, which dictates where your power should be (if on the indoor bike trainer).

STRENGTH-TRAINING WORKOUT (see workout, page 38)

❺ <u>Friday</u>

SWIM 2:00

- 400 S – 200 K – 200 P warm up, continuous
- 12 x 25 with: 10; alternate build up – build down – easy – fast
- 2 x 100 easy with: 15
- 4 sets of: 500 L1 with 30 second
- 10 x 50 L2 with 10 second
- 100 easy with 15 second
- 12 x 50 with: 10 cool down

RUN 0:30

- Easy recovery at L1.

❻ **<u>Saturday</u> – brick; look for improvement over this workout last cycle (the preference is to do this workout through the night to get used to riding and running at night with some sleep deprivation).**

BIKE 3:00

- L1/L2. Putting in the time. Focus on "going the distance" today.

RUN 1:30

- L1/L2. Putting in the time. Focus on "going the distance" today.

BIKE 2:00

- L1/L2. Putting in the time. Focus on "going the distance" today.

RUN 1:00

- L1/L2. Putting in the time. Focus on "going the distance" today.

❼ <u>Sunday</u>

RUN Trails 3:00

- Steady L1/L2 effort. Just get used to slogging through it when the legs are heavy and fatigued from yesterday.

☑ **TRAINING PLAN FOR DOUBLE ULTRA TRIATHLON**
WEEK 12
TOTAL HOURS: 5:15 + 100-MILE/24-HOUR RUNNING RACE OR 24-HOUR BIKE RACE

Training Zones
L1: 55–70 percent Max HR
L2: 65–78 percent Max HR
L3: 76–86 percent Max HR
Sweet Spot: 75–88 percent Max HR
L4: 84–92 percent Max HR
L5: 90–96 percent Max HR
L6: 93–96 percent Max HR
L7: Max Effort; HR insignificant due to short nature of efforts

❶ **Monday – DAY OFF**

❷ **Tuesday**
SWIM 0:30
- 6 x 100, alt S-K-P continuous
- 16-20 x 50 L1 with: 10 (3 Swim – 1 Kick)

BIKE 0:45
- Aerobic recovery at L1

STRENGTH-TRAINING WORKOUT (see workout, page 38)

❸ **<u>Wednesday</u>**

RUN 1:00

- Complete L1 recovery effort

❹ **<u>Thursday</u>**

BIKE 1:00

- Aerobic recovery at L1

❺ **<u>Friday</u> – TEST (best done at the track)**

RUN 1:15

- Warm up the first 15 minutes. Then complete 4-6x (build the curves – cruise the straights). Then take a couple minutes to get prepped for the test
- TEST: 5-mile aerobic TT. Set your HR monitor to beat three beats below and three beats above 75 percent (creating an effective 5-beat, non-beeping zone). Slow down or speed up accordingly when your HR monitor starts beeping. Get your mile splits as well as overall time to compare to future tests.
- Cool down the rest of the time at L1

SWIM 0:45

- 200 S-K-P Continuous
- 5 x 100 L2 with: 20
- 2 x 50 easy with: 10

❻ **<u>Saturday</u> – Race Day**

❼ **<u>Sunday</u> – Race Day continued**

☑ TRAINING PLAN FOR DOUBLE ULTRA TRIATHLON

WEEK 13

TOTAL HOURS: 16:15

Training Zones
L1: 55—70 percent Max HR
L2: 65–78 percent Max HR
L3: 76–86 percent Max HR
Sweet Spot: 75–88 percent Max HR
L4: 84–92 percent Max HR
L5: 90–96 percent Max HR
L6: 93–96 percent Max HR
L7: Max Effort; HR insignificant due to short nature of efforts

❶ Monday

Swim — L1 easy recovery

❷ Tuesday

BIKE 2:00

- Warm up the first 20 minutes
- Main set: 4 x 15 minutes L3 with 10 minutes easy L1 between; strong and steady.
- Cool down the rest of the time at L1

RUN 1:15

- Warm up the first 10 minutes. Then hold your HR at L2 for the middle 55 minutes. For the final: 15 of

every 5:00, surge to L5 (3K-5K race effort), then settle back into your aerobic pace. This is to help with leg turnover speed and lengthening your stride.
- Cool down the rest of the time at L1

STRENGTH-TRAINING WORKOUT (see workout, page 38)

❸ Wednesday

RUN 1:30

- Steady L1/L2 aerobic run over rolling hills.

BIKE 1:30

- Aerobic recovery at L1

❹ Thursday

SWIM 1:30

- 400 S – 200 K – 200 P warm up, continuous
- 12 x 25 with: 10; alternate build up – build down – easy – fast
- 2 x 100 easy with: 15
- 6 x 500 with 1:00; desc 1-3, 4-6 as L1/L2/L3
- 500 Kick L1
- 500 Swim L1

❺ Friday

BIKE 3:00

- L1/L2 ride; easy pressure on the pedals. Keep HR below 70 percent, which dictates where your power should be (if on the indoor bike trainer).

❻ **<u>Saturday</u>**

RUN Trails 5:00

- Just put in the time. Keep it aerobic and don't overstretch yourself.

❼ **<u>Sunday</u> – DAY OFF**

☑ TRAINING PLAN FOR DOUBLE ULTRA TRIATHLON
WEEK 14
TOTAL HOURS: 24:00

Training Zones
L1: 55–70 percent Max HR
L2: 65–78 percent Max HR
L3: 76–86 percent Max HR
Sweet Spot: 75–88 percent Max HR
L4: 84–92 percent Max HR
L5: 90–96 percent Max HR
L6: 93–96 percent Max HR
L7: Max Effort; HR insignificant due to short nature of efforts

❶ Monday
SWIM 0:45 complete L1 recovery; your choice
BIKE 0:45
- Aerobic recovery at L1

STRENGTH-TRAINING WORKOUT (see workout, page 38) **– include 5 minutes of jump rope**

❷ Tuesday
BIKE 2:00
- Warm up the first 20 minutes
- Main set: 3 x 20 minutes steady L3 with 10

minutes easy L1 between. Strong and steady.
- Cool down the rest of the time at L1

RUN 1:15

- Warm up the first 10 minutes. Then hold your HR at L2 for the middle 55 minutes. For the final: 15 of every 5:00, surge to L5 (3K-5K race effort), then settle back into your aerobic pace. This is to help with leg turnover speed and lengthening your stride.
- Cool down the rest of the time at L1

❸ **Wednesday**

SWIM 1:00 complete L1 recovery; your choice

❹ **Thursday**

SWIM 2:00

- 400 S – 200 K – 200 P warm up, continuous
- 12 x 25 with: 10; alternate build up – build down – easy – fast
- 2 x 100 easy with: 15
- 3 sets of: 500 S L2 with 1:00
- 400 K L2 with: 30
- 300 P L1 with: 30
- 200 IM L2 with: 30
- 100 Choice L1 with: 30
- 5-8 x 100 with: 15 (25k-s-k-p), cool down

RUN 1:15

- Steady L1/L2 aerobic run over rolling hills

❺ <u>Friday</u>

BIKE 2:00

- L1/L2 ride; easy pressure on the pedals. Keep HR below 70 percent, which dictates where your power should be (if on the indoor bike trainer).

❻ **<u>Saturday</u> – brick; look for improvement over previous attempts (do the workout over the night time).**

BIKE 3:00

- L1/L2. Putting in the time. Focus on "going the distance" today.

RUN 1:30

- L1/L2. Putting in the time. Focus on "going the distance" today.

BIKE 2:00

- L1/L2. Putting in the time. Focus on "going the distance" today.

RUN 1:00

- L1/L2. Putting in the time. Focus on "going the distance" today.

❼ <u>Sunday</u>

BIKE 6:00

- Steady L1/L2 effort. More important to put in the time than to press the effort. If you find yourself "driving" the effort, pull back just a little bit and keep things light.

☑ TRAINING PLAN FOR DOUBLE ULTRA TRIATHLON

WEEK 15

TOTAL HOURS: 19:45

Training Zones
L1: 55–70 percent Max HR
L2: 65–78 percent Max HR
L3: 76–86 percent Max HR
Sweet Spot: 75–88 percent Max HR
L4: 84–92 percent Max HR
L5: 90–96 percent Max HR
L6: 93–96 percent Max HR
L7: Max Effort; HR insignificant due to short nature of efforts

❶ **Monday**

SWIM 1:00 easy L1; your choice

STRENGTH-TRAINING WORKOUT (see workout, page 38) **– include 5 minutes of jump rope**

❷ **Tuesday**

BIKE 0:45

- Aerobic recovery at L1

❸ **Wednesday**

RUN 1:30

- L/1/L2 strong aerobic effort over rolling hills. Press the effort on the up and cruise on the down.

BIKE 2:00

- L1/L2 relaxed aerobic. If you find yourself pushing the effort, pull back and settle into light pressure on the pedals. Use 70 percent HR as the ceiling of your effort.

❹ Thursday

SWIM 0:45

- 1,800-2,000 straight at L1. Get into a rhythm and hold steady the whole time.

BIKE 2:00

- L1/L2 relaxed aerobic. If you find yourself pushing the effort, pull back and settle into light pressure on the pedals. Use 70 percent HR as the ceiling of your effort.

STRENGTH-TRAINING WORKOUT (see workout, page 38) **– include 400 Hindu Squats**

❺ Friday

SWIM 2:00

- 400 S – 200 K – 200 P warm up, continuous
- 12 x 25 with: 10; alternate build up – build down – easy – fast
- 2 x 100 easy with: 15

- 2 sets of: 800 L1 with 1:00
- 4 x 100 K L2 with: 15
- 400 L2 with 1:00
- 8x50 L1 non-free with: 15
- 1,000 pull L1
- 300 swim L1

RUN 0:45

- Easy recovery at L1

❻ Saturday

RUN 2:30

- Warm up the first 15 minutes. Then hold your HR at L1-2 for the middle 2:00. Negative split your effort over a rolling course. Punch it up and over 10 of the shorter hills – efforts of around 30-45 second – with varying amounts of settling back into L1-2 between these punctuated efforts.
- Cool down the rest of the time at L1

❼ Sunday

BIKE 6:00

- Strong L1/L2 ride. In the second half, complete 3 x 40 minutes L2 with 15 minutes easy L1 between. The L2 should be done at the strongest aerobic effort you can hold for the full 40 minutes. Stay aerobic here, though.
- Cool down the rest of the time, easy L1

☑ TRAINING PLAN FOR DOUBLE ULTRA TRIATHLON
WEEK 16
TOTAL HOURS: 21:00

Training Zones
L1: 55–70 percent Max HR
L2: 65–78 percent Max HR
L3: 76–86 percent Max HR
Sweet Spot: 75–88 percent Max HR
L4: 84–92 percent Max HR
L5: 90–96 percent Max HR
L6: 93–96 percent Max HR
L7: Max Effort; HR insignificant due to short nature of efforts

➊ Monday – DAY OFF

➋ Tuesday
RUN 0:45
- Aerobic recovery at L1

BIKE 0:45
- Aerobic recovery at L1

SWIM 1:00
- Aerobic recovery at L1

❸ Wednesday

SWIM 2:00 complete L3 5,000-6,000 straight swim

BIKE 0:45

- Aerobic recovery at L1

❹ Thursday

RUN 0:45

- L1/L2 effort. Relaxed, just put in the time. Finish with 5x (20 second strides – 1:40 easy)

BIKE 0:30

- L1 recovery, soon after running

❺ Friday

SWIM 0:45

- 400 swim – 200 Kick – 200 Drills
- 4 x 25 on: 30 (build up – build down – easy – fast)
- 100 easy
- 5 x 50 at 76-86 percent with: 10
- 500 done as (25K – 25 right arm – 25 left arm – 25 swim), easy L1
- Cool down until you feel relaxed and loose, then get out.

❻ Saturday

BIKE

- L2 – 9-10 Hours. The goal to get comfortable on being in the saddle for a long time.

❼ **Sunday**

- L1/2 – 4 hour trail run – the legs will be tired, just get through the run. No problem if the run is cut short.

☑ TRAINING PLAN FOR DOUBLE ULTRA TRIATHLON

WEEK 17

TOTAL HOURS: 23:00

> **Training Zones**
> **L1: 55–70 percent Max HR**
> **L2: 65–78 percent Max HR**
> **L3: 76–86 percent Max HR**
> **Sweet Spot: 75–88 percent Max HR**
> **L4: 84–92 percent Max HR**
> **L5: 90–96 percent Max HR**
> **L6: 93–96 percent Max HR**
> **L7: Max Effort; HR insignificant due to short nature of efforts**

❶ Monday

SWIM 1:00 easy L1; your choice

STRENGTH-TRAINING WORKOUT (see workout, page 38)

– 5 minutes of jump rope

❷ Tuesday

BIKE 2:00

- Warm up the first 30 minutes
- Main set: 2 x 30 minutes L3 with 15 minutes easy L1 between. Strong aerobic to tempo effort, working on getting in a groove more than forcing the pace/effort.

- Cool down the rest of the time at L1/L2

RUN 1:15

- Warm up the first 10 minutes. Then hold your HR at L2 for the middle 55 minutes. For the final: 15 of every 5:00, surge to L5 (3K-5K race effort), then settle back into your aerobic pace. This is to help with leg turnover speed and lengthening your stride.
- Cool down the rest of the time at L1

❸ <u>Wednesday</u>

RUN 2:00

- L1/L2 effort. Relaxed, just put in the time.

BIKE 0:30

- L1 recovery, soon after running

STRENGTH-TRAINING WORKOUT (see workout, page 38)

500 Hindu Squats! Go for it and see if you can do it

❹ <u>Thursday</u>

SWIM 0:45

- 1,800-2,000 straight at L1. Get into a rhythm and hold steady the whole time.

BIKE 1:30

- L1/L2 ride; easy pressure on the pedals. Keep HR below 70 percent, which dictates where your power should be (if on the indoor bike trainer).

❺ **Friday**

SWIM 2:00

- 400 S – 200 K – 200 P warm up, continuous
- 12 x 25 with: 10; alternate build up – build down – easy – fast
- 2 x 100 easy with: 15
- 4 sets of: 400 pull L1
- 8 x 50 L2 with 10 second
- 200 IM L2 with 30 second; done as 2 x 100 IM continuous
- 100 easy with 15 second
- 12 x 50 with: 10 cool down

RUN 0:30

- Easy recovery at L1

❻ **Saturday – brick; look for improvement over this workout last cycle (do the workout overnight).**

BIKE 3:00

- L1/L2. Putting in the time. Focus on "going the distance" today.

RUN 1:30

- L1/L2. Putting in the time. Focus on "going the distance" today.

BIKE 2:00

- L1/L2. Putting in the time. Focus on "going the distance" today.

RUN 1:00

- L1/L2. Putting in the time. Focus on "going the distance" today.

❼ Sunday

RUN 4:00

- Steady L1/L2 effort. Just get used to slogging through it when the legs are heavy and fatigued from yesterday.

☑ TRAINING PLAN FOR DOUBLE ULTRA TRIATHLON

WEEK 18

TOTAL HOURS: 12:00

Training Zones
L1: 55–70 percent Max HR
L2: 65–78 percent Max HR
L3: 76–86 percent Max HR
Sweet Spot: 75–88 percent Max HR
L4: 84–92 percent Max HR
L5: 90–96 percent Max HR
L6: 93–96 percent Max HR
L7: Max Effort; HR insignificant due to short nature of efforts

❶ Monday – DAY OFF

❷ Tuesday – DAY OFF

❸ Wednesday

SWIM 0:30; your choice, complete L1

BIKE 0:45

- Aerobic recovery at L1

❹ Thursday

BIKE 1:00

- Aerobic recovery at L1

STRENGTH-TRAINING WORKOUT (see workout, page 38)

❺ **Friday**

RUN 1:00

- Complete L1 recovery effort

SWIM 0:45

- 200 S-K-P Continuous
- 5 x 100 L2 with: 20
- 2 x 50 easy with: 10
- 600 pull at upper L1
- 4-8 x 50 with: 10 cool down, your choice

❻ **Saturday**

BIKE 6:00

- Steady L1/L2 effort – more important to put in the time than to press the effort. If you find yourself "driving" the effort, pull back just a little bit and keep things light.

❼ **Sunday**

RUN 3:00

Just put the time in. Cut back or omit depending on how your legs are feeling.

☑ TRAINING PLAN FOR DOUBLE ULTRA TRIATHLON
WEEK 19
TOTAL HOURS: 15:30

Training Zones
L1: 55–70 percent Max HR
L2: 65–78 percent Max HR
L3: 76–86 percent Max HR
Sweet Spot: 75–88 percent Max HR
L4: 84–92 percent Max HR
L5: 90–96 percent Max HR
L6: 93–96 percent Max HR
L7: Max Effort; HR insignificant due to short nature of efforts

❶ Monday
SWIM 1:00 easy L1; your choice

❷ Tuesday
BIKE 2:00
- Warm up the first 20 minutes.
- Main set: 3 x 20 minutes upper-L2 with 10 minutes easy L1 between. Apply strong aerobic effort, working on getting in a groove more than forcing the pace/effort.
- Cool down the rest of the time at L1

RUN 1:00

- Warm up the first 10 minutes. Then hold your HR at L2 for the middle 40 minutes. For the final: 15 of every 5:00, surge to L5 (3K-5K race effort), then settle back into your aerobic pace. This is to help with leg turnover speed and lengthening your stride.
- Cool down the rest of the time at L1

❸ <u>**Wednesday**</u>

RUN 1:00

- L1/L2 effort. Relaxed, just put in the time.

BIKE 0:30

- L1 recovery, soon after running

❹ <u>**Thursday**</u>

SWIM 0:45

- 1,800-2,000 Straight at L1. Get into a rhythm and hold steady the whole time.

BIKE 1:30

- L1/L2 ride; easy pressure on the pedals. Keep HR below 70 percent, which dictates where your power should be (if on the indoor bike trainer).

❺ <u>**Friday**</u>

SWIM 1:15

- 400 S – 200 K – 200 P warm up, continuous

- 8 x 25 with: 10; alternate build up – build down – easy – fast
- 2 x 100 easy with: 15
- 20 x 100 with: 15 (2 at L1 – 2 at L2 – 1 at L3)
- 12 x 50 with: 10 cool down

RUN 0:30

- Easy recovery at L1

❻ <u>Saturday</u>

BIKE 4:00

- Aerobic all the way; L1/L2, more about putting in the time than making it a workout. Finish feeling refreshed.

❼ <u>Sunday</u>

RUN 2:00

- Steady L1/L2 effort. Stay fresh on your feet.

☑ TRAINING PLAN FOR DOUBLE ULTRA TRIATHLON
WEEK 20 – RACE WEEK
TOTAL HOURS: 6:15

Training Zones
L1: 55–70 percent Max HR
L2: 65–78 percent Max HR
L3: 76–86 percent Max HR
Sweet Spot: 75–88 percent Max HR
L4: 84–92 percent Max HR
L5: 90–96 percent Max HR
L6: 93–96 percent Max HR
L7: Max Effort; HR insignificant due to short nature of efforts

➊ Monday – DAY OFF

➋ Tuesday
SWIM 1:00
- 6 x 100 continuous, alt 100 S-K-P; 2nd set of 3 faster
- 6 sets of: 150 pull at L1 with: 20
- 100 kick at L2 with: 15
- 4 x 50 swim descend 1-4 from L2 – L4 with: 10
- 200-500 cool down, your choice

❸ Wednesday

RUN 1:00

- Easy aerobic effort; keep your HR at L1 for the first 35 minutes. Then finish up with 5x (:20 strides with 1:40 easy jog).

BIKE 1:00

- Easy aerobic effort; keep your HR at L1 for the first 45 minutes. Then finish up with 7x(:20 spin ups with 1:40 easy spin).

❹ Thursday

SWIM 0:45

- 6 x 100 continuous, alt 100 S-K-P; second set of three faster
- 4 sets of: 150 pull at L1 with: 20
- 100 Kick at L2 with: 15
- 4 x 50 swim descend 1-4 from L2 – L4 with: 10
- 100-200 cool down

BIKE 1:00

- Warm up the first 15 minutes
- Then complete 4x(2:00 at L3 with 3:00 easy L1 recovery); in control, without maxing out your effort.
- Cool down the rest of the time, easy L1

❺ Friday – **DAY OFF**

❻❼ <u>Saturday/Sunday</u> – Race Day – Huge Test

It's going to be a long race, but you've prepared well. Ride the highs as long as you can and push through the lows — they will come but they will also pass. Keep your HR well in control on the swim and bike — mostly below 70 percent — so you have the legs for a solid run each day. Spin at 90-100 rpm on the bike on flats and spin at 85 + rpm on climbs. This will help save your legs for the run as well. Don't be afraid to start the run easy and play it conservatively as you want to make sure you finish strong. That's where you can make up gobs and gobs of time on those who started out too aggressively. Good luck!

TWITCH TIPS

1. *Focus on completing 85 percent of the workouts, with the goal to complete each exercise in just a few minutes.*
2. *Don't overanalyze the process — KISS*
3. *Adjust your workouts constantly to add new variety/challenges to avoid mental "burnout."*
4. *Make sure you spend time training overnight several times before the race to familiarize yourself with how it will feel race day.*
5. *Adding multiple discipline "brick" workouts are great confidence boosters in your training.*
6. *Remember, the race will come down to the run — save your legs for a strong finish!*

CHAPTER 5 – WAYNE'S TRAINING TIPS

"Training gives us an outlet for suppressed energies created by stress and thus tones the spirit just as exercise conditions the body."
- Arnold Schwarzenegger

Now you've got your training program outlined. How can you better maximize the experience? The following is a compendium of some of my blog posts from Endurance Racing Report (http://www.enduranceracingreport.com) written to help you take full advantage of your training regime.

Mix Up Your Training Routine
We have all been there, lots of training miles and some mental/physical burnout in our specific sport disciplines. Consistently training over a series of weekly training blocks is so important for the best opportunities for a strong race performance. There

is a "fine-line" of being over-trained. Sometimes it makes sense to add some variety for a workout or two just to mix it up and keep the mind and body fresh. For example, after 16-20 weeks of training with a mix of intervals, long endurance days, hill-climbing strength workouts (bike and run) — it's fun to change the normal schedule. This always happens to me when it's 90 degrees. Being on the East Coast, of course, we have 90-percent humidity as well. When you're outside in the middle of hot summer weather, it's sometimes hard to keep the mental focus for another long weekend workout.

I have personally found value in adding completely different routines just for a few days then get back to the focus of the race-specific training. Like most athletes, I would much rather be outside training, but on those rare occasions when the motivation is low, especially when it's freezing cold/dark outside, at 4:00 a.m., sometimes a change is in order. There are many DVDs available that cover topics such as indoor cycling, running, core, strength training, pylometrics, etc. These DVDs are inexpensive and can be added to your normal training schedule to give you some additional variety.

The use of a combination of training aids; such as, the standard jump rope, indoor bike trainer and a room for floor work is all that is needed to have a challenging and beneficial workout. Of course, the bike trainer could be replaced with a rowing machine, treadmill, ski machine, etc. — you get the point.

Here are a couple of programs to check out that I use regularly, and of course, there are plenty of others: *Cyclocore, CycloZen , Run-nerCore, Spinervals*, and the killer workouts from *Insanity* (the workouts have direct impact on my cycling power as measured by increases on the power meter — check it out) and P90X. If you have any workout programs that you feel have a "cross-over" benefit, please email me, as I always like to see what else is working for athletes, at wayne.kurtz@racetwitch.com.

The following workout is one of my favorite training workouts. Give it a try for some fun and variety when it's one of those stressful workdays, brutal weather, and/or you just need a change in the routine (even if you're a runner and/or triathlete, etc., there are good crossover benefits):

Cross Training Workout:
Forty-five Minutes of Insanity (pick any of the DVDs) in the kit — they are absolutely brutal; you

could use whatever you like that offers a full-body workout with strength, pylometrics, power yoga, but needs to have cardio as a key feature.

Followed by:

- 65-minutes biking on the trainer with the following set:
- 10 minutes at 75 percent target heart rate, minimum 90 rpms
- Five minutes steady jump rope (use a mat for cushion to prevent shin splints)
- 20 minutes at 80 percent target heart rate, keep up the rpms
- Five minutes easy spinning
- 5 x (three minutes big gear at 85-90 percent, two minutes recovery very easy spinning)

Followed by:

Fifteen minutes snowshoe hill-climb running repeats (for those of you who have snow). Do a series of as many repeats (recover on the downhill) with a steep trail hill. If no snow, grab the trail shoes. I am not a huge fan of the treadmill, but you could easily do the same hill repeats on the treadmill with a high-elevation setting.

Of course, training outside is where we would most train, but don't discount the indoor workout. If you plan it out with variety, it won't be the same old boring workout (especially sitting on the trainer for hours). The above workout will definitely make you "feel it" the next day and most importantly have fun!

Wayne's Favorite Body Weight Strength Exercises
Many of us incorporate strength training during pre-season for preparation of the upcoming racing season. It's always important to remember that intensive strength training (especially with the use of weights) should be reduced as the mileage and intervals are increased in preparation for the racing season. For example, during pre-season training, strength training might include three to four sessions per week and will reduce to one to two sessions per week to ensure recovery for the specific sport discipline training. The various Internet websites (YouTube) make it very easy to review the exercises to ensure that you have the correct form. For those with iPhones, check out a nifty application called iFitness and has over 230 exercises with videos, descriptions and daily log.

Here are my top 10 (body weight) strength-training exercises (no machines necessary):

1. Hindu Squats – Great quad power builder and aerobic work – build up to 200 or more reps! Check out link for description: http://www.mattfurey.com/hindu_squats.html.

2. Squat Thrusts – These are killer – see if you can build up to 75-100 (fast but good form) http://exercise.about.com/b/2005/02/23/exercise-of-the-week-squat-thrusts-2.htm.

3. Wall Sit – Build to two minutes: http://exercise.about.com/od/exerciseworkouts/ss/howtosquat_8.htm.

4. Pushups – There are so many different ways to do them, check out this site to get up to 100 pushups, www.hundredpushups.com, try pushup jacks (search on web).

5. Plank – Build up to hold for three minutes and your abs will be very strong: http://www.abs-exercise-advice.com/plank.html.

6. Jump Rope (speed sessions) – Build up to five minutes. I just love this jump rope and watching the best – Buddy Lee (amazing!): http://www.buddyleejumpropes.com.

7. Reverse Crunch – Build to a set of 50: http://www.ehow.com/video_4433370_

do-reverse-crunch.html.

8. Mountain Climbers – Build up to 100 total (50 for each leg): http://www.ehow.com/video_4433370_do-reverse-crunch.html.

9. Supermans – Build to a set of 20 "holds:" http://www.criticalbench.com/exercises/supermans-exercise.htm.

10. Bicycle Crunch – Build to one minute (fast and high rev's per minute), http://www.ehow.com/video_2351933_bicycle-crunch-exercises-abs.html

Of course, there are so many exercises to add to your strength sessions. Try the above set two times through and you will enjoy the "burn!"

Five Training Thoughts

1. Make sure you have a goal at the beginning of every training session. This will provide focus for the workout versus just slogging through some miles. We all know this, and I am as guilty as everyone else to just put in some miles for any of the various disciplines. Of course, easy aerobic days are necessary for recovery sessions, but I think if we all look at our training schedule, we tend to lack enough high-quality workouts.

2. Get away from all the technology for a few days: no heart-rate monitor, watch, cyclocomputer, GPS, etc. Just go out with a goal in minutes on a different route than normal. Don't worry, not monitoring average mph, watts, heart-rate average, calories burned, miles, time, etc. will be OK for a few days!

3. For each of your workouts for a week, consider adding an extra 10 percent of additional time on each workout. For those of you who adhere to number two (above) without all the "tools" just do a normal route and add some more distance. It's surprising to me that just by adding such a small amount of time per workout can have significant benefits in overall fitness (consistently over a six-week period).

4. For the hard bike or run session of the week (OK, yes it's fine to pull out the technology tools for this session) set a baseline distance to evaluate in six weeks. For example, the five-mile run at 80 percent target heart rate used to monitor in the future or hill repeat on bike or run — set a baseline and monitor in six weeks for next test.

5. After the specific training session, write down the following:

a. Three things that you did well for the workout.

b. Based on the session what do you need to improve?

c. What is the one thing you could do differently that could help make the most improvements?

Hill Repeats – Add to Your Daily Workout Schedule
Running and biking hill repeats can offer significant improvements to your racing even if your key races do not involve all climbing. Spring is a great time of the year to add the workout into your training program. How many times have we all read about the benefits of adding hill repeats to our training and say, "I have to add some hill training to my program," and never get around to it? It seems every magazine, book, coach, etc. discusses the benefits of adding these to the overall program. They are brutal when you first start them after the off-season. However, the benefits of gradual progression with hill repeats, enhances the aerobic engine (aerobic, anaerobic), power, overall body strength and mental toughness.

You will definitely uncover your weaker areas during these workouts. When running hill repeats it's important to maintain good form and "lean" into the hill and remember to use your core muscles.

A strong arm drive while running will also help get you to the top a bit quicker, but it will raise the heart rate quickly into the "red-zone" area. While biking, fatigue will set in the upper body and will be an eye-opener, and remind us if we spent enough time with strength training in the off-season.

After four to six weeks of consistent weekly hill repeats, it's amazing how much running/cycling strength improves each workout. Of course, mix them up to add some variety. Here a few that I like to incorporate into my program:

1. Biking or Running – During an aerobic workout, push every hill to the top and then recover and get back to aerobic heart-rate zone.

2. Mountain Bike – Pick a hill that takes around three to five minutes to climb and start with a series of five hill repeats and build over time. I like to add the mountain bike, as it's pure quad power (no standing) with upper body strengthening, balance and technical skill benefits.

3. Running workout (roads or trails) – Find a hill that will take around five to seven minutes to climb but not so steep that it's hard to keep up a pace. After a solid 15-20 minutes to warm up, start small with three to five hill repeats and recover with an easy jog down the hill. Add three minutes hard-level running after the recovering jog (down the hill) on one or two of the reps and no recovery — just head straight back up the hill. Incorporating this hard-level running then automatically going back uphill without recovery will trash the legs, so start slow and make sure you finish the workout.

4. Killer Combined Bike/Run Hill (repeat workout) – Either mountain bike/trail running or road option. I like to find a shorter hill and a bit steeper than the longer gradual climbs for this workout. Start with good 20 minutes of warm up with some short pickups then do one to two minutes climbing on the bike — standing only first set then seated while clicking into harder gears while climbing in the second set, coast down to the bottom and quickly change to running shoes and focus on a quick turnover while climbing. Yes, you need a safe place to ditch the bike while running! Recovery-jog back to the bottom and repeat. Start with two to three sets (one bike-climb and one run-climb is one set) and get up to 10-15 after some weeks of progression. This is an unbelievable workout with numerous benefits for racing.

The Brick Workout – Variety for Endurance Athletes
The brick workout offers many benefits for triathletes and multi-discipline endurance sport athletes. As Wikipedia states: Triathletes train for this phenomenon through transition workouts known as "bricks": back-to-back workouts involving two disciplines. For most triathletes the normal brick is to combine a bike followed by run workout to simulate race conditions. I am not sure how brick derived its name for the workout, but I just assumed it was that your legs feel like they have bricks in them when you begin running immediately following a bike ride.

It is a key workout many triathletes use to simulate the feeling on running with tired legs. Many of you know what the feeling is like the first mile or two during an Ironman Distance Triathlon when you fly through the transition area and head out on the run. I add different bricks to my normal training program to "mix" it up and not just do the same bike/run bricks. They all have the benefit of training the body and mind to push through fatigue.

Here are a couple different bricks compared to the normal bike/run to add some variety to your training:

Swim/Bike – This workout is an important transition that is often overlooked by many of us. Swim 3,000-4,000 meters straight swim (the last 500 meters pick up the pace to be faster than race pace), get out of the water, and immediately get on the bike and ride 75 miles above (Ironman Triathlon race pace).

Run/Swim – This workout is tougher than you think. Run three to four hours (marathon pace) on trails (carry a pair of swim goggles with you) and end the run if possible at a pool/lake and swim a set of 5 x 500 meters at Ironman swim pace. Make sure you keep up the electrolytes, as it's easy to get those nasty calf cramps in the water!

Triple brick – This is one of my favorites to build mental strength to push through tired legs. Bike three hours hard pace and immediately follow with 1,000 Hindu Squats (yes, your quads will feel like mush), then head out to a two-hour run on trails. The final 30 minutes of the run, do 10 hill repeats (steep and short). These final hill repeats will be brutal, but if you can build up to 10 over a period of time the long-term strength benefits become significant and can help when you need to push at the end of race during the run.

There are so many versions of brick workouts. Consider different varieties to keep it fun! The brick workout's benefits are immense for all endurance athletes.

Junk Miles Are Not Always Bad

How many times have we all heard for years that it's all about quality, quality, quality miles? It continues to be an ongoing theme for years, and I disagree that "junk miles" have no benefits, and we should just take the day off. In my opinion, the term should be changed to "recovery" miles. As we all know, the key to an effective long-term training program is to balance hard efforts with recovery sessions to continuously "tear down" and rebuild key muscles for specific sport disciplines. If you experience an injury, be smart and cross train on the recovery-mile session with a different sport discipline.

Moving back to the goals, each of us should have a focus of each workout. It might be any of the following: negative-split workout, hard intervals, long-slow distance for building endurance, hill repeats, etc. However, I feel that the "day off" is not mandatory as many athletes won't workout on Friday so they save themselves for the long weekend workout, key speed session, etc. If you keep the heart rate in the 50-65 percent of range of (lactate threshold), there is no reason to always take off Friday. The session might only be 30-45 minutes of very easy spinning on the bike, swim or running, yoga — and it keeps the body "fresh." The body acclimates to working out every day. Of course, there are days when life gets crazy and we have to take a day off or we take time off for an injury. It's an active recovery and not just "junk miles." Personally, I train seven days a week – and it works for me.

Consider adding recovery miles to the day(s) that you normally take off, especially if time allows later in the day after a race. As we see with the Tour de France cyclists, they ride on days off of the Tour. There are benefits of flushing the legs and body with recovery miles.

Weekend – Running Hill-Repeat Workout!
For those of you not racing over a weekend and want a different hill-repeat routine, try this workout to test your engine. This workout builds leg and lung power, and several weeks of consistently doing the workout will improve your hill running and result in power increases in the legs.

Find a hill that is a steady climb that will take between six and nine minutes in duration while keeping your heart rate in the 85-95 percent range of lactate threshold. So you will not be "red-lining" the heart rate but training right in the "sweet spot." The hill should not be so steep that you can't maintain the heart rate in this range. It can be done on trails or roads (I prefer roads).

After a 10-15 minute warm up including five 20-second "pickups" start the first set:

1. Climb the hill and keep your heels down (so you don't aggravate your Achilles) while pumping arms. Focus on solid breathing and staying in your heart-rate zone.

2. Recover on the run down (should take you roughly the same time as going up).

3. When you reach the bottom, then start performing 50-75 Hindu Squats (error on the low side for the number of squats). If you need a demonstration of a Hindu Squat, check out video on www.racetwitch.tv or do a Google search and you will see plenty of examples on how to do it correctly. Hindu Squats should be done quickly and exploding up, but stay under control with good form.

4. After Hindu Squats immediately head back up the hill for the second set.

For those of you who want a challenge, attempt the following set:

Eight to 10 hill repeats followed by 175-200 Hindu Squats after each recovery downhill run. Alternatively, do half of the hill climbs and Hindu Squats with nose breathing only — this is very tough but teaches you how to belly breathe and stay relaxed!

After completing your set, warm down with 20-30 minutes of running in the 65-70 percent heart-rate zone.

I love this workout — and I do it every week (mid-week), because the benefits are immense! Please let me know your thoughts.

Top 5 Challenges To Add To Group Bike Rides

The weekend is time for the long training ride with a group of friends. In most cases, the rides have one main goal, which is to do over-distance training with some tempo riding or significant accelerations up the hills. Over the years, I have learned a few different ideas to spice up the miles and keep it challenging but not to turn every ride into a "slug fest time trial." Here are my five challenges to consider for your weekend group rides:

1. Signs – The sign game should begin about a third of the way into the ride so everyone is warmed up — and the key is to sprint to specific signs. For example, a township, county or state road sign that is along your route. Define the specific signs before hand, but it's up to each individual to spot the sign in the distance and then begin the sprint.

2. Road Kill Sprint/Jumping – This involves looking for road kill in the distance (the road in the lane you're riding so be safe), which in my area could consist of dead raccoons, deer, groundhogs, opossums, etc. — and the goal is to have everyone sprint to the road kill and the leader must successfully jump over the road kill. No scraping the back wheel on the animal allowed and focus on being safe for the jump over the road kill!

3. Big Chain Ring Climbs – These consist of several long, gradual or short, steep climbs preferably during the second half of the climb when the legs are getting tired. The goal is to have everyone shift into the big chain ring and climb the hill. The main focus is just to get to the top no matter how long it takes to crest the hill.

4. Big Chain Ring Total Rides – These rides are best when all the riders have plenty of miles of training during the season. It's a difficult workout — and if your legs are not strong, there will be plenty of suffering. Pretty easy concept, everyone in the group shifts to the big chain ring and is not allowed to be in the small ring for any part of the ride. The climbing can be very tough!

5. Hill Climbs – Pretty basic; it's a sprint for everyone to see who can climb the hill the fastest. There is one twist to make it fun and embarrassing. The winner of every climb is required to circle back down the hill and laugh at everyone suffering to the top and will receive the added benefit of another hill climb.

I hope you try some of these challenges to keep it interesting for everyone! For more ongoing information, don't forget to check out www.RaceTwitch.com.

TWITCH TIPS

1. *Head to the hills to increase power and strength.*
2. *Add Hindu Squats as the aerobic and power benefits from this simple exercise are immense. You can do them anywhere.*
3. *Create your own workouts by mixing up various training techniques.*
4. *Don't underestimate the value in intervals and speed training as part of your overall program.*
5. *Follow the rule of Gradual Progression to eliminate potential injuries. Build up your training hours over time.*

CHAPTER 6 – RACE SPECIFICATION TRAINING – GOING SOLO

"Each player must accept the cards life deals him or her: but once they are in hand, he or she *alone* must decide how to play the cards in order to win the game." ▪ Voltaire

Your comfort and success come race day will be enhanced by incorporating race-specific training to mirror the terrain or conditions of your upcoming race. What you wear and the type of gear selection matter, but also you need to ensure your training routine also prepares you to deal with the terrain-specific challenges you might encounter. As we all know, don't try new products, clothes or equipment for the first time on race day.

The benefits of pre-race planning are immense so there are no surprises on race day. How many times have you been in a race and even with all the various details on race websites with regards to elevation gains, heat, number of aid stations, etc., do you hear the comment: "I was not aware that the race had so many hills!"

Race-specific training can include many of the following:

- Heat training/acclimating
- Hill training
- Downhill running on trails
- Roads versus trails (running and cycling)
- Training in the aerodynamic position for a triathlon versus in an upright position (so your back does not spasm)
- Learning how to walk fast in multi-day running races or the long run is important — especially with a race like the Deca Ultra Triathlon, which is 262 miles, and a long way to go. Learning how to walk quickly for long distances is imperative for this race.
- Training without headphones (biking and running) where it's not allowed in the race

There are many more, but one that is often overlooked is training solo.

TWITCH TIPS

1. *Training solo will build confidence and mental strength come race day.*
2. *Take the DNF (Did Not Finish) out of your vocabulary. Unless you face a major injury, you will get to the finish line no matter what.*
3. *Remember every "low" during a race will go away eventually, and you will get back to a better energy level.*

Of course, training with others is enjoyable, but if you're competing in a long race, mental strength becomes extremely important. The benefits of training alone for some of the long-distance training will pay off come race day when you experience the "lows." In many cases you will be alone without another athlete anywhere in close proximity.

Social training is great, but in many cases athletes become "too" comfortable in having the security of another friend when training. When it's race day and you are facing a "bonk," a mechanical problem with the bike, blisters, etc. you know what happens? Yes, some athletes will "crack" mentally, and they end up on the DNF (Did Not Finish) list. I have seen this happen so often as athletes get so comfortable talking through the early miles of a long race with friends to make the "miles go by quickly" and then late into the race they have no mental strength to get to the finish when they are on their own.

As you all know, the "real" race for most athletes begins late into the race. For example, during a 100-mile running event, the "real race" begins at mile 80-85, and in many cases, it's all about your ability to push it hard to pass fellow competitors and finish strong while running alone. It's no different in an Ultra-Distance Triathlon where the later stages of the run will be the most difficult.

TWITCH TIPS

10 Must-Have Items for an Ultra-Distance Triathlon

- *Duct Tape*
- *Bag balm*
- *Arm warmers*
- *Race nutrition strategy*
- *Headlights*
- *Sunscreen*
- *Small knife*
- *Rain gear for crew*
- *Warm clothes*
- *Garbage bags*

I don't want to discount the fun of training with others, but if you prepare for your races with various race-specific training techniques, make sure you learn how to train alone to build your mental strength to get through the "lows" on your own! In Chapter 4, I highlighted training sessions that should be done overnight so you get used to cycling, running and sleep deprivation, and these should be done alone.

CHAPTER 7 – MENTAL PERFORMANCE TRAINING TECHNIQUES

"Ralph Waldo Emerson once stated, 'A man is what he thinks about all day long.' He understood an important principle that is at the heart of success for that matter. If you believe you are going to be successful, achieve your race goals, and think about succeeding day in and day out, you will succeed. Unfortunately, the reverse is equally true."
- Wayne Kurtz

Do you realize your mental training is just as important as your physical training? Yes, that is right. Mental preparation is equally if not more important than physical training. How many gold medalists do you think won their medals by thinking, "I can't do this?" I bet if you were to ask any of them what was in their heads during the competition, most, if not all, would say it was about pure focus on the end goal — to win. They did not allow their minds to be cluttered with negative thoughts and "can't dos." So, as you embark on your course of training for an Ultra-Distance Triathlon, be aware that your ability to stay mentally in the moment; stay positive and work through the lows.

So many athletes and coaches talk about the importance of mental training but actually have no recommended strategy or plan similar to the normal physical training program that I have outlined in Chapter 4. The first step is to clearly define your goals in writing. I recommend that you not only look at the goals every day, but also write them down every day.

Race Goal Setting

By writing down your goals at the start of a buildup for a key race, reinforces it in the subconscious. You might think it's crazy, but the process of not only writing down the goal at the beginning but at least writing (not just reviewing) it down on paper

TWITCH TIP

Repeat after me: I will write down my goals every day.

at least once per week adds to the reinforcement process.

One of the strengths of many athletes is the mental capacity to push on when times are tough during a race. I've developed the following process, that if used regularly and consistently, can be highly effective. It only takes a few minutes in the beginning to establish the goals then just a few minutes per day for evaluation of the workout.

- Clearly establish the race goal including race date (for your key race) and write it in your training log.
- What are your three biggest strengths and three biggest weaknesses (or sacrifices) with respect to your goal (in terms of achieving the goal)?
- Create a simple "identifying statement" about yourself of what it's going to take to be successful in the race. Very basic — I use the following and it's "engrained" in my head: *I will persist until I succeed.* Make it short and memorize it.

Please print out several copies or just keep a file on your computer and include it as part of your recording process (with training log). It's a great tool to refer to and see how you're progressing with training. At most, it will take a few minutes to complete.

Post Workout Evaluation – answer these questions at the end of every workout every day:

- What two aspects of the workout went well today?
- Based on the workout, what areas do I need to focus on improving?
- What can I do differently in future workouts to achieve my goal?

There is no question athletes who have a strong, stubborn, continuous drive and race-day visualization embedded into their subconscious have an advantage come race day! I have seen many less "pure-athletic-ability" athletes outperform many faster athletes with mental strength (yours truly being one). I am by no means athletically gifted in any of three disciplines (just consistent in each); but by following specific mental training techniques throughout my training program/race day, I have achieved solid results by finishing strong when other excellent athletes pushed too hard in certain conditions of a race and ended up struggling to the finish line. (Yes, I have been there as well and have experienced times when getting to the end was brutal!)

Some personal examples include managing a top five finish in my first Deca Triathlon; and achieving top three and fifth places in Double Ultra Triathlons by following a specific race-day mental strategy. Yes, things can happen and don't always go according to plan on race day, but overall, the key is to maintain a consistent mental focus. A solid mental training strategy will provide a process to get out of the significant "downs" that feel like they last forever during a long race. Also, mental toughness will be extremely important for the later stages of the run, which is where the real race begins.

As a **Certified Performance Edge Coach** and trained by Dr. JoAnn Dahlkoetter, author of *Your Performing Edge*, I have added additional clarity and structure to my personal training program. I also go out of my way to assist other athletes with mental-training strategies. I combined excellent training and knowledge gleaned from Dr. Dahlkoetter to perfect strategies — and you can do the same for your own mental training program. The key is consistency when it comes to mental training during your daily workouts. It builds confidence going into the race. You spend 15 minutes day —

that's all for six weeks prior to your big race. You will remain much calmer at the start — and trust me, the results can be amazing! Yes, it really works!

I also like to address the challenge of staying focused when you're involved in events of this duration. You will feel particularly challenged to "stay in the moment." What I like to do is break a race down into its sections (swim, bike, run), and then keep my mind focused on just that part. For example, the swim is all about thinking about only the swim. Do not start getting out ahead of yourself and trying to consider what comes next and how to cope with it. Instead, think of each condition as a small race. For example with a Double Ultra Triathlon, I break the swim into 45-minute segments (this is normally when I grab food/drinks, etc), the bike is normally broken down to 100KM sections and the run is every 30KM.

Create a mindset around that smaller race. Visualize and focus on finishing each as a micro race. It works great — and I learned the hard way. My first experience with the Double Ultra Triathlon, I kept taking on thoughts about the enormous magnitude of the forthcoming miles/kilometers I faced in each discipline. This "over-thinking," if you will, knocked my concentration off and caused distractions to remain focused for such a long period of time. I kept thinking too far into the future especially during the bike when I was about halfway through — and my mindset was thinking of the run already! You know what I've already said about distractions and what that can cost you during an event.

Mental Visualization (credit: *Your Performing Edge*)
Create a picture in your mindset of one of your greatest race performances and bring all five senses into the visualization:

- What did you see when you started the swim?
- How about the sounds during the race?
- What did you smell at the aid stations or biking through the countryside?
- What feelings did you have with your hands on the handlebars, the lightweight almost no feeling of your feet landing on the ground during the run?
- What competitors did you focus on during the swim, bike and run?

Capture this perfect race performance and write out a quick summary to answer all the questions.

Name of Race:

Venue (Place) of Race:

Date and Time of Race:

Distance of Race:

Type of Race (sport, short or long, hilly):

Temperature and Weather of Race:

Wind Speed/Direction:

Your Final Time:

Your Split Times for each part:

Your Finishing Position (Overall, Age-group):

Your Pre-Race Routine: Describe your feelings and behavior during the pre-race warm-up period.

Was your warm-up period satisfactory? If not, how might it be improved?

Describe Your pre-Race Food:

How long was your meal before the race?

Were you satisfied with the food you ate during your evening meal and morning snack before the race? If not, how might this have been improved?

What were your plans (strategy and tactics) before the race?

Did you actually use these tactical plans during this race?

Were you sufficiently rested before this race? If not, what would you like to do differently?

Where were you positioned (in relation to your other important competitors) during the beginning, middle and end of this race?

At what point during the race did you first start feeling tired?

At what point during the race did you feel the most tired?

Were you fueling your body adequately during the race? What could you do to improve this?

What was your Energy-Fatigue Index (Rate 1-10, With 10 = feeling the best, 1 = lowest energy):
Pre-Race:
Start:
Mid-Race:
At the Finish:
After:

Other than simply "going faster," what could you have done to improve your performance in this race?

What did you learn during this race that may help you to improve your performances during future races?

What could you do differently in your PHYSICAL training that would help to improve your next race performance?

What could you do in your MENTAL training that would help to improve your next race performance?

Name, date and distance of your NEXT race:

What are your mental and physical training plans to work toward that race?

What are you goals for your next race?

What are your goals for the remainder of the season?

Take this race visualization and recreate it for your current upcoming race. Every evening before going to bed, just visualize the perfect race performance identifying how you will feel; and what things will you say to yourself during the race to keep your focus. Create a few power keywords about your strengths such as "I will persist until I succeed," "I feel light and fast," or, "I will stay in the present." Create your own mental keywords of what you can use come race day.

BEGINNING YOUR VISUALIZATION

Take these simple steps

(credit: *Your Performing Edge*)

Relaxation and Breathing – Lie down for best results.

Centering – Breathe in through your nose, focus on your center out through your mouth, relax and let go.

Imagery of Peak Experience – Go through your peak experience — present time — before, during, after.

Senses – Bring in all your senses for each part.

Anchoring – Create a color, shape, a word or gesture — something to remember your experience by.

Come Back into the Room – Slowly – feeling refreshed, recharged, alert and awake. When you are ready, open your eyes.

Wayne Kurtz's Mental Training Tips

A couple of mental training tips I use during a race, include:

Cycling – I learned over the years of racing in these Ultra-Distance Triathlons that by just saying a mental statement to myself, "Stay on the bike." and, "Beefy Ice will make me feel nice," works like magic. These personal affirmations repeated help especially when energy levels drop. More about the "Beefy Ice" in Chapter 9!

Running/Biking Mental Technique – The Rope/ Magnet Technique – This strategy is highly effective during the later stages in the run or bike sections of the race. I call it my "rope technique." Other experts call it the magnet concept. It's a very simple concept that has worked for me for years. The technique can be implemented when you are at a crucial part of your specific race. Focus on a competitor that is in front of you that you can see up the road, and imagine this person has a rope around his waist and his energy is pulling you along.

The other thought is to think of the person with a magnet on his back, and you are "sticking" to them. Envision the magnet pulling you toward them. It might sound crazy if you have not practiced this basic mental-training technique, but it works! Just focus on the competitor and create a mental vision of them pulling you along.

If you tell yourself that they are doing all the work and use their energy to keep you maintaining their pace. Practice it regularly and you will see the results, especially late into a race when you are pushing the pace. Of course, you can call it something else and create a picture of anything to have the same benefits of using a competitor's energy to pull you along. The next thing you know you will be passing them!

Wayne's Top Three Extreme Mental Preparation Strategies

Use these strategies to incorporate into your training. These strategies should not be taken lightly. Start them gradually in terms of the total duration.

Bonk-Run Strategy: Plan on a slow run for several hours (four to six hours) and the key is to only drink water and some electrolyte capsules (carry food, gels, bars, etc.) during the run. Determine how long it takes (in hours) until you get very low on energy because of lack of calories — and then learn what it "feels like." Eat, drink calories immediately to recover and regain energy. See how long it takes you to get back to a normal running pace again. This simulation of being in a bonk-down state trains your mind and body of what it will feel like potentially come race day. Of course, when finishing this run, rehydrate, drink your recovery drinks/foods immediately after finishing.

Stomach Distress Strategy: For those of you who have experienced gastro intestinal distress during a long race, it's tough mentally to get back when the body and mind feel so bad. This technique is very brutal, but the goal is to stimulate stomach problems so you know how to deal with it. For those of you who never get stomach distress, I am jealous! The specific technique is to eat and drink items right before a run or bike that you know your body does not handle well. For example, I cannot eat yogurt or chocolate before a run or I will be in the bathroom for sure. So, what I do is to eat these items and force stomach problems in the bathroom (yes, this is brutal and sounds crazy and pretty nasty), but then I see how long it takes me to get back to a normal running stride and feeling good again. It's purely simulation on how you will handle it if you have gastro intestinal problems during an Ultra-Distance Triathlon.

Blisters Strategy: You must know how to handle blisters if you're susceptible to them in very long running races especially if you attempt the Quintuple or Deca Triathlon races! It's important that you learn how to fix your feet early. What is the specific item you will use to treat blisters? Is it temporary or sometimes a nagging pain that cannot stop you unless very severe and infected? Don't ever drop out of a race because of blisters, the pain is temporary but not finishing lasts forever! Also, the longer races may not only involve more blisters but severely swollen feet and numbness.

Wayne's Mental Strength Training Workouts

Long Indoor Bike Ride – As I have outlined in the training schedules in Chapter 4, plan on doing several very long rides on your indoor training. I learned this technique from an excellent European athlete who regularly rides 12-17 hours on the indoor bike trainer to prepare his mind for the long hours biking around a 1.2-mile loop of the Deca Triathlon. Riding indoors can be very difficult mentally to stay on the bike and just keep spinning the legs with no coasting.

Long Distance Race Strategy (100-mile example) – Consider running a 100-mile or 24-hour running race with one key objective: finish the last six hours very hard. The key is to conserve your energy as much as possible during the early hours and get your mind focused on a very strong push late into the race. This technique will build mental strength to learn how to finish strong and run hard with significant fatigue.

Visualization – When you are training, visualize how you will feel during the race. Also, focus on checking in with your body to make sure you focus on breathing from the core and relaxing.

Post-Race Suggestion – After all the months of building up to one of these races and the commitment required, I feel it's important to celebrate your success by having something as a reward a few weeks after the event. For example, it could be having a nice dinner with a spouse or family, going to a favorite destination for a day or two, making a financial purchase of something of interest, spending an evening with friends and enjoying a glass of wine, attending a future RaceTwitch Club Meet-Up and share your experience, etc. The key is to reward yourself (it does not have to be a monetary expense) and create a sense of accomplishment.

CHAPTER 8 – INTERNATIONAL RACING AND THE FAMILY

"Memorize and follow this never-fail recipe; get started. Don't quit." ▪ Barbara Winter

Until you've been intimately involved with athletic events, you may not realize that some sports more so than others create a tight family atmosphere. The lines between family and friends begin to blur and despite what may seem like an obvious competitive situation, you will find — especially in Ultra-Distance Triathlons that take place often over the course of several days — that family members, who come out to support athletes, form not just tight bonds with other families but also with competitive athletes. You can't help but become close when drawn together by common interests and goals. And these same interests keep you together in this kind of community where people really spend serious time getting to know each other, connecting, and supporting each other. It's really quite something – and for newcomers it's an unexpected treat to build often-lifelong friendships and to find that perhaps desired self-made "family" where you feel comfortable and accepted.

Ultra-Distance Triathlons are also evolving into a unique cultural experience. It's interesting that over the years that while the Ultra-Distance Triathlons originated in the United States, European-based events and athletes now dominate the sport. Of course, Americans still participate (yes, I am one of them) and love these races. In fact, I have personally taken it upon myself through books like this one and my website and blog to spread the word about these amazing events and the families, crews and community behind it. With folks like myself evangelizing the experience and its power to change lives, I hope to draw in many more passionate athletes and get them to consider training for and participating in these long races.

As I mentioned in the opening, the races offer a great venue to create a sense of community. Europeans in particular really leverage this opportunity. When events take place in local towns or cities, residents come together to support the race. Race directors, athletes and local families take a great deal of personal pride to show off their city or town to the competitors much like you see when the Olympics come to a certain city around the world only this is on a smaller scale.

Races hosted in Germany, Slovenia or Hungary, just to name a few, create fun, festive and infectious atmospheres. City officials and local businesses offer local cuisine, entertainment, etc. Athletes and their supporters can also enjoy the local culture, which enhances the overall experience even more. And the festival-like atmosphere is further encouraged with often-extravagant opening and closing ceremonies that include local media, incredible displays like skydiving shows, musical entertainment and more.

GLOBAL EVENTS

The good news for Ultra-Distance Triathlon enthusiasts and newcomers, sure to become hooked on the events, is endurance sports are rapidly growing worldwide — and the same is true of the IUTA Ultra Triathlon races. Starting in 2011, there will be many races added to the IUTA calendar to provide a total of 10 being held in Spain, United States, Austria, Hungary, Germany, UK, Slovenia, Switzerland and Mexico. The expansion will open new opportunities since many of the current races have been filling up quickly. Expect this expansion to continue as more athletes globally become involved in the sport — and further exposure in the media and through word of mouth attracts more athletes to join in the challenge.

Athletes who love to travel, especially to some places "off the beaten path," you can leverage the events being held in so many wonderful countries to do some amazing sightseeing. I suggest you plan some vacation time in and around the race events held in the various countries to really experience the culture and scenery. It can also give you some much-needed time to rest and recharge if you schedule your plans for after the event. Many race directors will also plan group excursions or provide advice on must-see attractions and landmarks in specific cities or countries.

Athletes, for whom international travel is not the norm, may feel trepidation and nervousness about

TWITCH TIP

Plan vacations well in advance or well after the race.

leaving the country — especially if they plan to travel solo. First, if you are new to the sport with no international travel experience, make sure you get a passport. Now let me assuage any fears you may have. I know you might be worried about language barriers, cultural differences or even political problems, but let me be the first to reassure you by experience, it will be fine. Embrace the traveling experience. Many times I mention to other athlete's considering traveling to a destination race that, "You just have to go with the flow." Everything will work out but you need to be open-minded and flexible.

Many race directors take personal responsibility by working with their staff to ensure your safety and comfort. They will coordinate airport pick up and drop off at the proper venues, including car rental locations and hotels. This effort helps eliminate problems with reading traffic signs, driving directions, GPS in another language, etc. They will also help with monetary exchange and provide translators if necessary. The race directors are in a sense an athlete's personal concierges.

A FAMILY AFFAIR

As I said, these events build a community of interest and create long-lasting friendships. This family atmosphere is common at almost every event I've ever attended — and every athlete is a part of that greater family that includes directors and volunteers.

As an example, I want to share an experience I had during an event. It occurred in the Bonyhad, Hungary Double Ultra in 2009. My wife and I arrived in Budapest. We did not receive all of our luggage from New York, which included bike, gear, specific race-day food, etc. The driver from the race that was transporting us to the race site coordinated solutions in the local language with the airline to track down luggage and alternative gear supplies. We had arrived several days early for the race and had enough time to wait; but we were not sure when the missing luggage would arrive.

Well, after several days and no luggage, but fortunately enough time to plan for the race without my gear, a local volunteer drove us two hours to

TWITCH TIP

Always arrive early to a race to ensure you have time to get items that might have been lost.

a large sporting goods store to purchase all the necessities, including running, cycling and swim gear. It was remarkable! And the race director offered bike, helmet, shoes, etc. just so I could race. So you now get an example of what I mean by *everyone is part of a family.*

The luggage finally arrived late the evening before the race, and of course, the volunteers again drove two hours with my wife to get everything at the airport. I put the bike together the morning of the race, unpacked my gear, and prepared for the race — and there is nothing like your own equipment, race-day food, etc.

Was this an unusual case? No, staff and volunteers routinely step up to assist when things go wrong. They want all participants (athletes, crew and families alike) to have a memorable and amazing experience. Whether things go perfectly or not, the race management's goal is for everyone to walk away with pleasant memories.

THE VARIABLES

Not all events are created equal. Variables in overall cost, vacation or holiday time off from work (for those who work), are different; but I promise that an international destination race will provide a lifetime of memories, and of course, a few new friends.

Here are five items to remember to enhance your international travels to a specific destination race:

1. Always arrive two to three days early to eliminate stress from unexpected problems such as lost luggage. It also gives you time to adjust to the new time zone and reduce jetlag.

2. Check with local officials to determine if there are any issues by bringing specific race-day energy foods through customs.

3. Get a complete understanding of the electrolyte drinks, food items, etc., that will be served during the race.

4. At the pre-race meeting if you have a question, just ask the race-director team. It always amazes me how many times athletes just don't ask for whatever reason.

5. Adjust to the local cuisine gradually prior to the race. I have seen many athletes who have experienced sour stomachs by not sticking to basic food items prior to the race. Experiment after the race — and of course, celebrate your great memories and race performance!

I could not write this book without mentioning a great friend, Guy Rossi from France (http://www.rossi.guy.free.fr). Everyone considers him the "legend" of our sport. He is well known throughout the Ultra-Triathlon family as an amazing and remarkable athlete. Guy's first sport was volleyball, and then he moved into triathlons at age 37 in 1985. Guy is 61-years-old now, and he is not slowing down at all with the amount of racing he does every year.

Guy will normally participate in all the IUTA World Cup races each year. I remember early on when I started in Ultra-Distance Triathlons, Guy telling me that I was going too hard on the bike, and of course, I just kept hammering on. Well, when Guy kept passing me loop after loop on the run, I learned a valuable lesson to make sure I save my legs for the run in the future. His experience is immeasurable within the Ultra-Distance Triathlon family.

Guy's remarkable lifetime Ultra-Distance Triathlon resume is like no other athlete:

- 53 Double Ultra Triathlons, best time 23 Hours, 21 minutes
- 27 Triple Ultra Triathlons, best time 40 Hours, 30 minutes

- 3 Quintuple Ultra Triathlons, best time 90 Hours, 57 minutes
- 10 Deca Ultra Triathlons, best time 9 days, 16 Hours (100 Ironman events in only 10 races)
- Ironman Personal Record: 10:29
- Marathon Personal Record: 2:55
- Guy has been on 18 podiums with IUTA Ultra Triathlons

CHAPTER 9 – RACE FUELING

"Food is your body's fuel. Without fuel, your body wants to shut down." ▪ Ken Hill

Our bodies need fuel — it's a basic fact. When we're involved in something as tremendously depleting to our systems as an Ultra-Distance Triathlon that involves miles and days of extreme demand on our bodies — it's imperative to have a nutrition strategy (preferably written so you will remember) for race day. It's not a time to experiment with different foods or liquids. When you commit to something as physically challenging as an Ultra-Distance Triathlon, it behooves you to not only train your body, and build your muscles and stamina, but also properly prepare to ensure you have essential foods and liquids with important electrolytes to keep you going and not put your health at risk.

Over the years, "race fueling" strategies have evolved and changed. Twenty-five years ago, I remember when race fueling consisted of bananas and water, with the occasional Gatorade if you were lucky to have some. I even recall an Ironman Distance Triathlon I participated in 20 years ago where it was hot — and the only liquid available was some warm Coke and water provided in cups beneath a box to provide shade. At that time, there were few volunteers — and what would be today considered prehistoric thinking about nutrition and race fueling, resulted in the provision of nothing more than what I just described. These conditions and beliefs about how one should fuel up and remain fueled during the race no longer apply and have been replaced with learned strategies to help

TWITCH TIP

Don't try a bunch of new race nutrition and/ or foods on Race Day! Yes, we all know it, but so many times athletes change midway through a long race, and all of sudden, try everything imaginable as well as whatever is at the various aid stations.

keep athletes in the best physical and mental shape possible to complete the race.

The Weak Point – Your Stomach

Perhaps your weakest point during the race can be your stomach. More specifically, a sour or nauseous stomach, which can bring you down mentally as well as physically. When you go through those stomach down periods, that happen throughout the race, you can prepare to deal with the problem effectively by coming prepared with the right blend of wholesome calories that keep your fuel at optimum levels. Just be aware, though, that no matter how prepared you are with your food and liquid strategies on the day of the race, unexpected exceptions can happen at anytime (e.g., flu) where its impact may require adjustments. You might want to have standby supplies for those occasions.

TWITCH TIP

Remember, it's so important to — no matter what — keep moving regardless of how slow your pace in any one of the disciplines (swimming, biking or running).

As outlined in the mental-training techniques chapter, the key to your continued success throughout the race is to keep your focus. Physical problems can distract. So anything I share will be aimed toward helping you refocus — and always, always keep moving forward. I am not going to get into all the various scientific evidence of what is the "best" race-day nutrition strategy for the appropriate amount of complex carbohydrates, proteins and fats, but I will offer thoughts on items to consider for Ultra-Distance Triathlons. For most athletes, who are preparing for a Double Ultra Triathlon, the fueling strategy can be very similar to a 100-mile running race with a few unique differences. It's important to get a handle on how many calories you expend per hour versus how many you need to keep your energy levels steady and keep the stomach and gastrointestinal system in check.

One unique factor, compared to a normal Ironman Distance Triathlon is that you will need to learn how to eat during the swim. It's a long time to be in the water, and the calorie loss can be immense. For the lake swims, there is usually a boat or a dock that can be used as a point to keep you nutrition supplies. Of course, with a pool swim, it's very easy as you can just keep everything on the deck at the end of your lane.

Wayne Kurtz's Double Ultra Triathlon Fueling Strategies
The point is not to tell you what I eat and/or drink, but I want you to use my examples to get an idea of amounts to consume during races. I follow a strategy of 400-450 calories per hour consistently for the entire race. I primarily use a specific formula of Hammer Nutrition Products, as they work for me. Use whatever works for you. I advise consistency from beginning to end. I believe consistency ensures you don't experience too many ups or downs during the race.

Pre-Race Morning – The very most I will eat is a Hammer Bar at least three hours prior to the race and drink a cup of coffee.

Special Provisions – I will take two to three Endurolytes (depending on the heat), one Amino capsule, and one Anti-fatigue capsule per hour

Swim – Every 35-40 minutes, I stop and consume Hammer Gel, Heed, Perpeteum and water.

Bike – I consume mainly Perpeteum, either measured out in a water bottle or in a pancake batter consistency in a gel bottle. I will normally consume a couple of ham sandwiches, a Hammer Bar, and an occasional Nutella, peanut-butter or banana sandwich.

Run – I will move the calories mainly to liquid form, which means I often consume mocha-flavor Perpeteum with caffeine, Hammer Gel and Heed. I will add Red Bull later into the run for a pickup to finish strong. Occasionally if it's cold weather, I will add warm chicken broth.

Ice – I am also a big fan of ice so if it's a hot day, I add ice in all bottles. For me personally, ice keeps my stomach cooler and helps to digest calories.

Deca Triathlon Fueling Strategies

This fueling strategy greatly increases calories. One item that is common for athletes, from post race

TWITCH TIP

If it's a hot race, purchase several insulated water bottles. They will keep the drinks cold, especially during the bike and run, and will save your crew from having to constantly refill bottles with ice. They work remarkably well! A must for the Deca in Monterrey when the temperatures can get very hot.

medical exams, is that body weight will remain relatively the same; however, body fat percentage drops significantly and muscle is converted to fat — especially with the Quintuple or Deca distances. I have a tendency to increase proteins in the very long races. The amount of calorie loss is enormous, so it's so important to have a specific strategy for nutrition — it's actually hard to overeat in the Deca.

Pre Race – Eat something light such as a bagel with peanut butter or Hammer Bar.

Swim – Every 30-40 minutes, eat various items such as Hammer Gel, Heed, Perpeteum, water, Nutella or ham sandwiches.

Bike – I use Pepeteum as the main fuel source, and I drink throughout the entire ride, but unlike a Double Ultra Triathlon that takes just a little more than a day, I have the tendency to eat a lot of real solid food. I will regularly eat rice, beans, chicken, of course Beefy Ice* or papaya. If I take a quick nap, I always will eat calories right before laying down.

Run – I will stick to mainly Hammer Nutrition liquids, but I will incorporate real food continuously through the race. Pizza with meat is packed with calories and offers consistent energy; I will eat it regularly. I will consume more caffeine as sleep deprivation becomes such a huge factor in the race. I also add liberal amounts of coffee and Red Bull!

Some of the most amazing things that I have seen athletes eat during long-distance triathlons include the following:

- Canned mackerel (my great friends from Sweden) during the swim
- Spaghetti with marinara during the swim in the Deca
- Non-alcoholic beer by the gallons or liters for the carbohydrates
- Nutella (served as a sandwich or just on the end of a spoon — simple carbohydrates)
- Sandwiches on the bike with ham, prosciutto, turkey and other protein meats
- Entire roasted chicken being eaten on the bike

***Wayne's Personal Secret Ingredient during the Deca Triathlon in Mexico: Beefy Ice!**

Just for background: During the 2009 Deca, we had several very hot days during the afternoons with baking sun. It was so important to increase

TWITCH TIP

Eat solid food choices during the bike, and then reduce it a bit for the run and look at a larger portion of calories from liquids.

liquids and overall calories to keep energy at appropriate levels. This race consisted of one Ironman Triathlon per day for 10 days consecutively. At one point, many of the athletes were suffering on the bike. I recall using some mental techniques and a personal affirmation: "*Stay on the bike no matter what,*" as I was positioning myself and moving up the leader board by making sure I kept on moving.

As I came around to the transition area, I yelled over to my great friend and Super Crew member, Rick Freeman, that I would like to have a cup of Mexican beef with ice. He looked at me strangely, along with every other crew, and asked, "Did Wayne say he needs Heed (Hammer Product that I drink regularly) with Ice?" So the next loop, Rick had Heed with ice, and I repeated, "No, I need Beef with ice." So next loop, I had a cup of mildly spicy Mexican beef with a bit of rice and ice mixed in. Does not sound too appetizing, does

TWITCH TIP

If you are own your own with no crew, clearly mark you food items in clear plastic containers so you can easily find the right supplements/powders/food and not waste time and frustration by digging through a bag in the middle of the night and not finding what you want!

it? It's not something you would find on the Food Network, but it worked. It kept the energy levels up, and the ice allowed my stomach cool in the extreme heat. Yes, it's my magic ingredient when I am feeling down in a very long race like the Deca in the heat.

And always remember, the key is *consistent calories* throughout the race.

CHAPTER 10 – RACE-DAY STRATEGIES

"While most are dreaming of success, winners wake up and work hard to achieve it." ▪ Unknown

Even in business, leaders recognize the value of writing a strategic plan for their future success. The same idea applies when preparing for an Ultra-Distance Triathlon. Just like any business leader, you must plan, strategize and come up with ideas and actions to address any kind of variable or unexpected moment. There are so many variances that can come into play at anytime during a race.

Remember, these races are long — and trust me, there will be times when things go wrong. You will most assuredly encounter feeling down during some sections that challenge you mentally and physically. The best athletes are coming to these events well prepared, having carefully considered the race from a holistic viewpoint and creating their own kind of strategic plan, or at least strategically considering everything to the best of their abilities. It's important to have several plans — Plan A, B, C because if things don't go according to plan you just drop to the next plan.

Setting Goals

I prefer to map out my goals on paper — and I encourage you to do the same. As you go about writing your goals, I suggest you consider 10 key areas, which are as follows:

Nutrition – How often will you stop to eat during the swim? Plan a strategy from the very beginning and stick with it.

Spare Bike – If you can drive to the race and have room in your car or truck, take two bikes/ extra wheels so if you experience flat tires or mechanical failure or fatigue because of the bike style (time-trial bike vs. a road bike with aero bars), you can easily change to another bike.

Lightweight Road Bike – If it's a Quintuple or Deca race, consider the advantage of using a lightweight road bike with aero bars and aero wheels for comfort over the fatigue from a steep-angle, time-trial bike. Comfort becomes more important over time,

TWITCH TIP 

Create a race-plan notebook or use a sample worksheet available on Racepeak.com.

and the key is to stay on the bike, no matter how slow a pace. Get on and off the bike as little as possible. Of course, if it's a very long race, you will need to get off for sleep breaks. This will have a significant impact on race performance.

Beware of the Chair – Don't get in the habit of sitting on a chair during the run section, no matter what. Also, make sure you don't waste unnecessary time in the aid station or transition area. Get your drinks and food and keep moving.

Create Your Mantra – Repeat these words in your mind: "I WILL STAY ON THE BIKE. I WILL KEEP MOVING ON THE RUN. NO MATTER WHAT."

Plan Speed and Sleep Goals – What's your average speed goal for the bike? Write out in your race-plan notebook where you want to be on the bike at specific distance checkpoints: 100K, 200K, 350K, etc. Also, what is your sleep strategy for the longer races such as Quintuple, Deca Iron triathlons?

Plenty of Running Shoes – Bring several pairs of running shoes, with each a half-size larger. This is especially important in a long race; such as, the Deca Iron. Feet swell significantly, and a change to different shoes, with an increased size, will relieve pressure on the toes, etc. For example, if your running shoes are normally size 9, then my recommendation is to take a pair of size 9.5, size 10, and 11. You can't believe how much the feet will swell — trust me I know it well!

Goal Pace – Write in your race-plan notebook what is your goal average pace for the run. Categorize your pace into two levels:

1. Goal pace

2. Race-of-your-life pace

Steady and Consistent – Focus on starting steady and remaining at a consistent pace. Avoid pushing too much through the early four or five hours of the race. Focus on staying in the moment. These races are long. Keep your mental state on what you're currently doing. Avoid focusing on too far in the distance or what you have to accomplish in the big picture.

Go Last Half Strong – Finish the last half of the run strong — no matter what the event distance. In most of the races, it comes down to the run. Athlete's who can finish strong, will have the greatest success. In the Deca, for example, it might mean just keep moving and not take additional stops and sleep breaks. The amount of time that can be made up is enormous by finishing strong.

Race-Day Goals

The race day is upon you — and you will want to have thought through your plans well in advance of the event.

First Aid for Your Feet – Know and be prepared to fix you feet from blisters, serious chafing, etc. It's important that, if you're susceptible to blisters when running, that you use a product such as Bag Balm/Glide or anti-friction creams to keep the friction and hotspots to a minimum. Fix your feet early on before they get too bad. Remember, no dropping out because of blisters — it's only temporary pain!

Grooming Basic – Make sure you trim your toenails. As your feet swell your toes may start to get close to the end of the shoe. It is easy to lose toenails for sure.

Diaper Cream – You're racing in a Quintuple or Deca; make sure you take some diaper cream.

It will cure significant chafing and rashes incurred by sitting on the bike saddle for hours.

Shelter and Comfort – Bring tents and sleeping bags for everybody, including your crew. Camping out can prevent long treks back to a hotel, inn or dormitory.

Plenty of Water Bottles – It's one of those items you can't have too many. Don't underestimate the amount of bottles that you will need for the bike and run. Label them to make it easy for the crew to mix and fill the right drinks per bottle. Also, sanitize the water bottles (your crew can help) consistently every day in a long race like the Deca to decrease germs and reduce the possibility of an illness.

Hand Sanitizer/Baby Wipes – Mandatory to reduce the amount of germs everywhere!

Key Swim Race Day Strategies

Target Your Swim – Take out the swim at a steady 70 to 75 percent HR target range. Remember, the race is never won during the swim section. Don't push too hard especially in a pool swim to sprint to pass individuals in your lane. Stay under control.

Carefully Consider Your Wetsuit – Since many of these races are in pools versus lakes, and may have a tendency to have warmer water, consider a short wetsuit versus long sleeves. You don't want to overheat under any circumstance, as it will take awhile to get the body back with consistent electrolytes.

Water Consumption – Make sure you drink more than water during the swim. Electrolyte replacement and calories are crucial.

Body Glide and Anti-Friction Cream – Make sure you have extra body glide or anti-friction cream available at the end of the pool or with your crew at a lake swim. These are long swims and the various anti-friction creams or products will eventually come off during the swim. This will eliminate the various wetsuit "burns" and sores that can occur from rubbing of the suit to the skin.

Lube Your Feet – Consider lubing your feet and a thin layer on hands, as they can get almost mushy and painful from being in the water for 4, 12, 20 hours for these races.

Key Biking Race-Day Strategies

Reserve Your Strength – Try to hold back during the first four to five hours and pick up the pace later into the bike section.

Lap Counter – For a long race, like the Deca Iron with 900+ laps on the bike, (Monterrey Deca), consider a lap counter. You can use a baseball-pitch counter so you can eliminate stopping and looking at the leader board. Also, mentally it helps to think in terms of laps vs. distance.

Bento Box – Invest in a Bento Box or a food box that fits on your handlebars near the stem. For very long races, it becomes extremely difficult to reach behind to your rear bike-shirt pocket to grab a gel or other food item. After a 24-mile swim, in the Deca for example, the shoulders will be very sore. Reaching for food becomes a painful experience until the shoulders begin to loosen up, which can take a couple of days.

Bike Lights – Have several bike lights and headlamps available. Do not waste time changing batteries.

Stay on the Bike – As mentioned above, the key is to stay on the bike as long as possible without stopping, so comfort on the right bike is very important. For example, if you have a time-trial bike and start riding in an upright position to stretch the back, etc.; the wrists can get very sore as compared to a comfortable hand position from normal road-bike handlebars.

Sunscreen – It's common sense, but so many athletes forget about sunscreen on the bike and just get fried. Load up on the sunscreen. With the long races you will be on the bike for several days.

Eat Constantly – Eat or drink calories constantly. If you start to experience a "down" point during the race, it is normally from a lack of calories. As I say to myself mentally on the bike, "Eating Beefy Ice will make me feel Nice!" (as outlined in race fueling strategy chapter — Beefy Ice).

Control Your Bike Gear Ratio – Keep your gear ratio under control and don't mash the gears and overwork the quads especially with the very long distance races.

Key Race-Day Running Strategies

Goal Pace Quickly – Get into you goal pace as quickly as possible and stay under control early on. The tendency is, that you will be so anxious to get off the bike and start the run, that many athletes start out too fast and just crush themselves and finish with a slow shuffle/walk.

Leader Board Time – If you are racing competitively, during the run is the time to start looking at the leader board to determine your race strategy to catch a competitor over time or hold off the competition. Your crew can help with this mental strategy especially if your mind is mush!

Eat and Drink Always – Yes, another common-sense item, but just do it. Eat or drink calories consistently over the entire distance of the run.

Caffeine – If you incorporate caffeine into the race nutrition, it's important to maintain it consistently so you don't crash.

Thoughts – Think to yourself, "Quick leg turnover."

Last-Half Push – As mentioned above, your best race performances will occur if you can push hard for the last half of the run. In most of these very long races, the majority of the athletes will be struggling at various sections during the run. Trust me, significant time can be made up or lost when you're running 84KM, 126K or 422K!

Moving and Moving – Keep moving and eliminate wasted time with unnecessary long times chatting at the aid station with crews/athletes.

Stomach Problems – Know ahead of time and get into the right mental state on how you will deal with stomach distress. What will you do to keep moving and pushing through stomach issues?

Your Feet – Remember, no DNF (Do Not Finish) for blisters — as mentioned above know-how to fix your feet!

The Shoe Rules – As mentioned above, consider changing shoes to a larger size when your feet swell to the point where your toes are hitting the end of the shoe.

Evolve Your Strategies
A simple way to look at your race strategies is to consider them a work in progress. Nothing is set in stone. As you begin your first competition, the strategies you develop for it may not work well for your second or even your third Ultra-Distance Triathlon. Listen to your body. Be open to adjustments and change. The bottom line is these races are hard. Few athletes would challenge that statement. So, be prepared to enjoy the high moments, but just

TWITCH TIP

Prepare various race plans; for example, Plan A, B, C. Everything will not go according to plan, and it provides a new plan immediately so you won't get down mentally as the race evolves.

realize you might have some lows too. Apply simple strategies, such as leveraging your crew. They can provide an outside viewpoint on your competitors and nudge you when maybe it's not so obvious to you that you need to refuel.

I have noticed over the years, as I have gained experience, that my racing strategies continue to evolve. There is no question that through experience — as is true of most things in life — you have a significant advantage, especially mentally for these types of races. As we've gone through, the key is to have your race-day plan (multiple plans to fall back on if things don't go according to plan), set your goals, make nutritional strategies, define your pacing, visualize your success, create positive outlooks, and define ways to manage the highs and lows. Then review your plan regularly so you create a mental picture in your subconscious. And just like your training-program strategy or daily workouts, make sure you have a race-day strategy to prime you for your ultimate athletic performance.

CHAPTER 11 – RACES FOR PREPARATION FOR THE EVENTS

"By failing to prepare, you are preparing to fail."
▪ Benjamin Franklin

Any athlete knows — especially when we're talking about such long distances — that one does not jump into endurance events without proper preparation and readiness. I'm sure what I'm saying is obvious to most of you reading this book. An Ultra-Distance Triathlon clearly with the distances involved in the swim, bike and run, is not for beginners who have never undertaken anything that requires this level of endurance and stamina just to finish. The rest of you who have done Ironman distance events have a small glimpse into the challenge — and the remainder of you who may have participated in longer ultra-running, cycling or adventure races have a clearer

TWITCH TIP

As a lifetime learner of endurance racing by continuously adding new races, techniques and training tips, I am always open to new thoughts and ideas. Please email me at wayne.kurtz@racetwitch.com with specific races you have considered for preparation for your Ultra-Distance Triathlons.

idea of what it requires to get in the best physical and mental shape to take on the challenge.

I strongly believe that with proper preparation and knowledge, you can take on an Ultra-Distance Triathlon and finish. How do you get started? Many athletes, who also wonder what type of race would best prepare them for an Ultra-Distance Triathlon. Now I can't answer the exact best race, but I can tell you what type of races to consider as part of your overall preparation for an Ultra-Distance Triathlon. Please realize, each athlete has strengths and weaknesses — so the key to success is to try to mix a variety of races that will have crossover benefits to the Ultra-Distance Triathlon.

The following are guidelines I've developed based on personal experience and trial-and-error at various events.

Three Key Races

I want to keep this process as simple as possible; therefore, I will focus on three specific Ultra-Triathlon race distances — and some races to consider during your preparation:

- Double Ultra Triathlon – Total time allowed to complete the race 36 Hours
- Triple Ultra Triathlon – Total time allowed to complete the race 60 Hours
- Deca Ultra Triathlon – Total time allowed to complete the race 336 Hours

The key for each of these races is to find a specific race that has similar amounts of total time. For example, for a Double Ultra Triathlon, look for a specific cycling, running, adventure or endurance race that will keep you out on the course for roughly the same amount of time. You will gain invaluable experience racing in similar long-distance endurance events where you'll uncover your own mental or physical highs and lows — and how to best manage them.

There is nothing like a race where you're experiencing side-by-side interaction with other athletes in a real competition versus another long training day. Your participation in a live race makes it real. It's not a simulation. It doesn't plug in guesswork. It gives you on-the-ground experience necessary to prepare for a live Ultra-Distance Triathlon.

Double/Triple Ultra Triathlons

There are many races to consider as preparation races. Of course, from a triathlon perspective, the Ironman Distance triathlon is a good preparation race with one addition. Since the Ironman Triathlon for many athletes will only require at least half of the overall time as a Double Ultra Triathlon, it's helpful to add some other options. For example:

Longer Workouts – Perform a long workout the day before the Ironman Triathlon. An example is a 6-8 hour bike ride followed by a 2-5 hour run at a steady pace. The next day for the Ironman race you will experience the similar tired legs as the Double/Triple Ultra Triathlon.

Extend Your Training Day – Taper going into the Ironman Triathlon and the day after the race make it a long training day — add a long ride of six hours or so.

Use common sense to avoid injuries — especially, if you're prone to running injuries in particular.

Preparation Running Races

The best running races to consider participating in to get comparable times at the Double/Triple Ultra Triathlons are as follows:

1. 24-hour running race (road or trail)
2. 100-mile trail or road race
3. A very difficult mountain running race that will take 20-plus hours.
4. Consider running back-to-back races. For example, a marathon followed the next day with an ultra marathon.

Of course, another alternative would be to do a longer run the day before the race, with the goal of just finishing the later miles/kilometers in the race at a hard pace. This will force you to learn how to run on tired legs. Keep in mind, most of the running is on roads versus trails for a Double/Triple Ultra Triathlon. Find races with similar running surfaces.

Preparation Cycling Races
Of course, the cycling section of the race normally requires the longest amount of time of the three disciplines, and it's important to spend long time periods on your specific race bike to be used in the Double/Triple Ultra Triathlon.

Many of the following races will get your "seat" prepared for hours in the saddle:

1. 24-hour road bike race
2. Double Century ride/race
3. Brevet Ride

Other races to consider for your preparation for the Double/Triple Ultra Triathlon include:

1. 24-hour adventure race
2. Long-distance snowshoe/cross-country ski race
3. A self-guided, long ride or run on trails
4. Long-distance, open-water swim race
5. Long-distance kayak/canoe race

Triple Ultra Triathlon
One key difference between the Double and Triple Ultra Triathlons, is the added element of sleep deprivation beyond 24 hours. Many of the races listed above can be extended and/or increased in

distance for a workout before the long-distance race. For example; instead of a 24-hour race, consider a 48-hour running or cycling race. The key is to get the body and mind used to handling the effects of pushing through sleep deprivation and the benefits of a short nap strategy versus without sleep.

Deca-Triathlon

The Deca-Triathlon has two different formats: the continuous format (all the swimming followed by biking and running); and the single Ironman distance format, which is one Ironman Triathlon per day for 10 straight days. Of course, both formats are difficult mentally and physically, with one key difference — sleep deprivation is involved with the continuous format.

In addition to long-distance endurance races outlined above, the best preparation for the Deca is to consider racing in several Double/Triple Ultra Triathlons, possibly a 6-10 day running race as well. The Quintuple offers a great starting point to get used to the significant sleep deprivation and significantly longer distances from a Double/Triple. My Ultra-Distance Triathlon race progression is not mandatory by any means, but just an example to consider if your goal is to finish the Deca. It is as follows:

Before my first Deca Triathlon, in addition to ultra-running/ultra-cycling races, I did the following Ultra-Distance Triathlons:

1. Finished five Double Ultra triathlons
2. Finished one Quintuple Triathlon

Personally, I believe in "gradual progression," which means I wanted to gain experience and learn how to race these events (not just finish) — and the confidence boost was significant by the time of the Deca. I not only finished the Deca on the first attempt, but also placed fifth overall. Much of my race strategy was acquired by the experiences in the other Ultra-Distance Triathlons.

The Deca Triathlon is considered one of the top 10 toughest endurance races in the world. It's an event like no other in my mind, and the difficulty level should not be underestimated. As mentioned throughout this book, with the proper mental/physical preparation and realistic time management, as outlined in Chapter 12; it's doable and you don't have to give up your job and family! The Deca finishing goal can definitely be a possibility! One key item to implement in your training for the Deca (continuous version) is to prepare for the very long run. Get used to walking/running for very long periods of time. As I mentioned earlier, racing a 6- or 10-day running race will prepare you mentally and physically for the demands of being on your feet for days in the Deca.

CHAPTER 12 – ENJOY THE CHALLENGE

"All endeavor calls for the ability to tramp the last mile, shape the last plan, endure the last hours toil. The fight to the finish spirit is the one ... characteristic we must posses if we are to face the future as finishers." ▪ Henry David Thoreau

The best piece of advice I can give you during your training and the actual participation in the Ultra-Distance Triathlon is to not get so caught up in the event that you lose sight of why you're doing it — whether that is for the mental or physical challenge or personal satisfaction of successfully doing something you never thought possible. And as you go through this often-arduous process, you may have some tough days with tired legs and a sore body. So I always encourage athletes to focus on the journey – the training one moment at a time, one triumph at a time — and of course, the actual race experience and achievement of your goal to cross the finish line.

I suggest you give yourself moments to reflect — timeouts to review your progress. Take this timeout after an all-night training session or back-to-back workouts. Manage your time effectively so that you can sit back, remember and reflect on your training — and time after the race too. One of the key components that I outlined in the Chapter 4 Training Programs is to keep the workout variety constantly changing to remain "fresh." With the vast amount of training hours required per week, it can be easy to get burned out later in the training program. Burnout before

TWITCH TIP

During a mental or physical low whether during training or race day, use a positive personal mantra to help discharge negative thinking.
Try something like this: "I love this sport. I feel great. I am strong and capable. I will finish no matter what."

you've even experienced an actual race is obviously not productive.

I want to share some key tactics to ensure you enjoy the challenge of race day. Make sure you have prepared your mind, as I have mentioned before, on how to handle the many challenges and difficulties that can happen during the race. The one thing you can be sure of is all the items you have prepared for will not always go according to plan. When you are "staying in the moment," during one of the three individual sections of the race, focus on smiling at times. This might sound crazy especially as mental and physical exhaustion sets in, but when you smile it's amazing that you will turn it around and feel better.

The Value of Camaraderie

As we mentioned, Ultra-Distance Triathlons create this amazing community of friends and family there to support the athletes. These friends and family will be there to encourage you — and it is this support that will give you a nice boost you when you might feel low. I also recommend you rely on your Super Crew, the folks you've assembled to help you through the event. While they're there to work with you and help out at critical points, don't forget to have fun with them too — this shouldn't feel like a job. Remember, they are there to assist you with achieving your race goals.

Not all athletes take this posture with their crews — and I have to tell you they're really missing out on a real bonding experience. Unfortunately, on a few rare occasions, I have witnessed an athlete yelling at his or her crew or race staff. While I find this unnecessary and certainly not productive, some athletes become more aggressive during the competition. I only hope that most crews realize this situation ahead of time rather than learning about it during race day; it makes it much easier for them not to personalize it.

Speaking of crews, since they can be so instrumental during a very long race and part of the great memories, it's very important for them to understand your preferences (race nutrition, goals, etc.) before the race. It's never a good thing for a crew to experience seeing an athlete (could be a family member) in such a bad physical or mental condition for the first time. The crew should understand how to best react to the situation. This is important to the athlete who intends to successfully finish despite such setbacks.

TWITCH TIP

A simple "thank you" to your crew throughout the race goes a long way toward building basic morale.

Do make a plan to address these problems and then review it with your crew prior to the race. The crew will know how to handle these challenges — and know where everything is located with respect to supplies (e.g., race gear, warm clothes for night sleeping when it gets cold, first-aid kits, etc.). You do not want your crew scrambling haplessly around when you need attention. Also, if you have a small crew, plan on a sleeping strategy for them for the long races too. Crewing for these very long races, like the Deca, are very exhausting on family/friends as well as athletes.

Embrace the Experience

The enjoyment for most athletes and Super Crews, alike, begins when race day starts. The months of training are over — and you're ready to confront your goals. Nothing reduces nervous anticipation and energy then reaching the day of the actual race. Your anxiety will reduce further the moment you're standing in the water, awaiting the gun to fire, and off you go.

As you participate in the actual race, relax and stay in the moment. Relax your mind. Don't get stressed out and rush through the transitions where you can make dumb mistakes; also, don't freak out if something happens. Remember, this race is long — and you need to keep focused for the long haul. You do have some flexibility, as 10 minutes lost in a transition during an Ultra-Distance Triathlon has much less impact than 10 minutes lost in a traditional Ironman Distance Triathlon. You have plenty of time and opportunity to make it up.

Enjoy and embrace the internal feeling of pushing yourself toward limits you've never experienced in shorter events. Use your crew's energy to drive you past difficult spots in the race. Create solidarity with your crew. Sometimes it's little

TWITCH TIP

Buy your crew a bottle of wine (if allowed) or a favorite food — and surprise them with it before the race.

things that build those relationships. So, don't get so focused you forget to reach out to your crew. Invite them to breakfast, lunch or dinner before the race — keep the banter light and fun.

Again, as I have mentioned before, if you are competing in your first Ultra-Distance Triathlon, it can be a life-changing experience for you and your crew. Many emotions can occur at the finish line – especially after overcoming the many challenges of these races. Many athletes feel the experience can be overwhelming and very emotional — the lifelong memories you build will fuel your desire to race again and again — and add more races to your calendar.

Remember: Smile at the finish line and have fun.

TWITCH TIP

Ten items to remember:

1. *Prepare before the race with your crew and review your race plans.*
2. *Don't dwell on situations that are not part of your plan.*
3. *Smile continuously especially when you feel bad, and of course, at the finish line no matter what.*
4. *Thank your crew.*
5. *Surprise your crew with a special food or treat.*
6. *Enjoy a meal with your crew for a very long event and talk about the experience so far!*
7. *It's OK to show your emotions and let go at the finish line with all the crews, family and other athletes!*
8. *Personally reflect on the race later after the race or the next day.*
9. *Write down the experience in your training journal so you remember what went right or wrong.*
10. *When you cross the finish line, carry something with you such as a country flag or item to be your "signature."*

CHAPTER 13 – RACES TO CONSIDER TO ADD TO YOUR DREAM LIST

"The only thing that will stop you from fulfilling your dreams is you." ▪ Tom Bradley

If there is one thing true about participating in the Ultra-Distance Triathlons is that you will definitely get to travel. The races are held throughout the world and give you the chance to extend your stay and really do some sightseeing, if you so desire. Also, when you're out in the field, participating in the actual event you will, without a doubt, witness some incredible countryside — not that you have time to sit and gaze at the scenery, but you will certainly have a firsthand glimpse of the people, places and environments.

Different from the large Ironman races, the IUTA race series includes several low-key, small town and larger world championship races. One major difference is that all the races have a family atmosphere, and it's very easy to meet some amazing people, different cultures, enjoy wonderful scenery, and make memorable experiences.

As I highlighted earlier, the majority of the races are held in Europe. New races continue to be added each year. Below I have highlighted several you may consider for your future "dream" races.

North America
Here are three races held in North America.

Tampa Double Ultra – This race is being held for the first time in March 2011. At the time of this book's production, it was not yet done so we don't have any notes regarding the event.

Virginia Double Ultra – Held each year in October, the Virginia Double Ultra offers athletes the choice of a Double or Triple Iron. Many athletes come back year after year to do the Double and then the Triple the following year. It's considered to be one of the most difficult courses because of the hills on the bike and run. Since the run and bike are held on loop courses, the hills will have an affect on your legs for sure!

Monterrey, Mexico, Quintuple, Deca – This race is also occasionally held as a Double Deca Iron. The Deca is considered one of the top 10 toughest endurance races in the world, and it's a goal many athletes will attempt to complete. The course is very fast (flat bike and run), contains well-directed courses, and offers normally nice weather (can get hot during the day and many times very cold evenings). It is a race like no other in my mind. It's very difficult, because of the race's long duration.

I recommend you don't underestimate the flat course as being easy. Racing day after day takes its toll. As I mentioned earlier, every other year, the race switches from a continuous format (swim followed by bike followed by entire run) to a one-Ironman-per-day format. A common question is: "Which is harder the continuous format or the one-Ironman-per-day format for 10 days?" The continuous Deca involves sleep deprivation and long times in each of the disciplines including the pounding for the very long run. However, with the 14-day limit to finish an athlete can have a bad day, sleep/recover, and come back the next day. The one-Ironman-per-day format only allows 24 hours each day to finish the Ironman. Therefore, if an athlete has a bad day (injury, sickness, etc.)

and can't complete the Ironman in 24 hours they are out of the race.

My personal opinion is that the continuous format is more difficult just because of the very long times in the saddle and run. Each format offers different difficulties, and as most athletes will state, "There is nothing like finishing the Deca."

IUTA Races

We want to give you a flavor of the various Ultra-Distance Triathlon races available at the time of this publication. If you would like to see actual race dates, please visit Race Twitch website at www.racetwitch.com, or IUTA at www.iutasport.com.

Lanzarote/Spain
Double World Cup Race
http://www.enduroman.com/

Tampa, Florida
Double World Cup Race
http://www.usaultratri.com

Neulengbach
Austria
Double World Championship
http://www.triathlon-neulengbach.at/

Bonyhad
Hungary
Double World Cup Race
http://www.ultraironhungary.com/

Lensahn
Germany
Triple World Cup Race
http://www.triathlonlensahn.de/

Lichtfield
United Kingdom
Double World Cup Race
http://www.enduroman.com/

Murska Sobota
Slovenia
Double World Cup Race
http://www.triatlon-ms.si/

Frauenfeld
Switzerland
Double World Cup Race
http://www.ultratriathlon.ch/

Lake Anna
Virginia USA
Double World Cup Race
http://www.usaultratri.com/

Monterrey
Mexico
Deca Iron World Cup Race
http://www.multisport.com.mx/

European Races

Like I said, you will have many travel opportunities — and most races are held in Europe. Here are some highlighted races for your consideration.

The Hungary Double Iron – This race offers athletes an amazing, festive atmosphere. The entire town of Bonyhad comes out to watch the athletes for up to 36 hours. There are local bands,

TWITCH TIP

If you have the vacation or holiday time, plan a tour through Europe that puts you in the race location at least two to three days ahead to ensure you can deal with any unexpected emergencies.

performers and dancers, authentic Hungarian food, amazing pre- and post-race celebrations. It's an incredible scene for a small town! The course is hilly on the bike and flat on the run.

Lensahn, Germany Triple Iron – This race has a long history with normally a larger field of athletes. It's considered a classic Ultra-Distance Triathlon as it has exceptional race direction, and the difficulty of the additional length with a Triple Iron. It's one of only two Triple Iron events held in the world. Definitely check this one out.

Murska, Sobota – For a fast Double Iron, consider Murska Sobota, Slovenia for a beautiful lake swim, completely flat bike course, and run course where you can definitely set a personal record. It's a small town atmosphere with a great festive feeling, with its local bands and cuisine.

Of course, each of these races adds something unique to your racing experiences — and each race should be considered part of your "dream-race" list, of course, that's my opinion.

As the growth continues with Ultra-Distance Triathlons internationally, more races will likely be added in the future. Enjoy the experience and spend some holiday or vacation days, in the specific race city and enjoy the local culture!

CHAPTER 14 – ULTRA-DISTANCE TRIATHLONS: YOU CAN PARTICIPATE – AND KEEP YOUR JOB AND FAMILY

"Most men lead lives of quiet desperation and go to the grave with their song still in them."
▪ Henry David Thoreau.

You've probably read up until now — and the primary question going through your mind is: "How in the world do you manage to balance an Ultra-Distance Triathlon with your family, career and personal interests?" Many athletes see it as a one or another proposition. It does not have to be. You don't have to sacrifice all areas of your life to serve your interest to compete in an Ultra-Distance Triathlon. You can, with proper planning, scheduling, and organization, balance all areas of your life — and still succeed in your desire to complete in one of these races.

So how does this work? Well, first allow me to dispel one important misconception. Many athletes mistakenly believe that with three specific disciplines (swim, bike, run) to train for that there isn't enough time for anything else, and most especially, there isn't enough time to maintain personal interests. Start by changing your belief about the time requirements. Do not consider training for an Ultra-Distance Triathlon as a full-time job. It doesn't have to be that time intensive. You can hold down a job, enjoy family time, train, and find time to have some fun. Second, if you have adopted the belief that this is a "job" of any kind, please stop. It shouldn't be viewed that way. While you need to exercise some commitment and time to make it happen, don't forget it's supposed to be a fun challenge — something you want to do. So don't turn it into something it's not meant to be.

You can figure out a well-balance training schedule that doesn't interrupt or disrupt work, family

Train late at night after your family goes to bed — and get the added benefit of simulating the actual environment you'll experience while racing.

and personal time. The traits – self-motivation, personal discipline and consistent behavior that will help carry you over the finish line – are the same characteristics that you need to achieve a well-balanced training schedule.

Recommendation number one: Schedule your workouts before the following week. Also, plan out your training schedule a week in advance. Sunday evening makes a great schedule-creation time. While working out your plan, evaluate your work and family schedule too. Work backwards. Plan your family and career time and then evaluate where in that schedule you can fit training time in. Don't be afraid to be precise about it. A tight but well-planned schedule reduces stress. You know what you're doing, and it doesn't leave an open-ended question about "when" you can do something. Also, be flexible and on the ready to make adjustments. Treating your schedule like it's set in concrete won't help your tension levels either. So, switch it up when necessary.

As I have outlined in Chapter 4, proper training workouts take about two hours per day during a standard week, which is definitely manageable. A good target goal is to keep the training consistent in the 15- to 20-hour range with a lot of variety and intensities.

Travel and Time Management

For those who travel frequently for business whether by air or road, time management will play a critical role in keeping your often-complex schedule on track. Personally, I travel a lot and have managed to build a strategy of training very early in the morning, as you never know how the day will go especially with flight delays and cancellations. As an example, here is a typical day scheduling for workouts when I am traveling with a flight at 7:30 a.m.

Wayne's Sample Travel Schedule

(Without overnight travel with workouts)

3:00 a.m. to 4:30 a.m.	Specific daily workout
4:30 a.m. to 5:15 a.m.	Shower, recovery drink, breakfast
5:15 a.m. to 6:00 a.m.	Drive to the airport
8:00 a.m. to 4:00 p.m.	Business and travel time
5:00 p.m. to 6:30 p.m.	Flight home

On the drive home, stop at a local "rails to trails" (running trail) for a quick 45-minutes to one-hour run (of course, having the "training kit"* in the car is helpful). You have to realize it's not impossible (as evidenced by my sample schedule); to workout while on the road. My normal training hours during a typical workday will range between two to three hours. Of course, if there is overnight travel, it's actually easier when you have a workout facility at the hotel.

Here are three critical tips:

Tip 1: Always, no matter what, take training clothing on all trips (even if they are not overnight trips).

Tip 2: Keep a standard training kit in the car (*running shoes, swimsuit, running shirt/jacket/hat/shorts, pair of biking shorts and helmet). The benefit of having the kit in the car is that if you have a long day of driving to meetings, you may pass a park (it might have a lake for swimming), ski resort that has bike rentals where you can get in a workout on the way back home. You need to think creatively when the schedule gets too crazy to fit in workouts.

Tip 3: Keep a jump rope and some stretch bands with you while traveling. And always get in some great strength and aerobic work using these tools.

Long Workouts and Family Time

Long workouts can interfere the most with your family time. How do you fit them in when you want to be with your family? Or most importantly you don't want to impose on your family so that they feel neglected or ignored.

Here is something you may not have thought about: Learn to train throughout the night! Your family time stays largely un-impinged upon – and you get the added benefit of training in an environment similar to race-day conditions. You will, after all, race in the dark and in many cases feel sleep deprived. It takes some time, but through gradual progression it's not hard to add night training to your weekly workouts and be functional at work if you do it during a weeknight. Of course, it's much easier to plan one day on the weekend for an "all-nighter." During the summer race season, when it's nice and warm in the evening, I will incorporate all-night training every week so it allows for time with the family and permits other interests.

TWITCH TIP

It's OK to miss a workout. Just ensure you don't miss the other 85 to 95 percent of your planned workouts.

A typical "all-night training" workout for me will look like the following:

Sample Night-Training Schedule

Friday After-Dinner Schedule (After Time for Digestion)	
10:00 p.m.	Multi-brick workout: four hours of riding; three hours trail run; two-hours riding; 1.5 hours (roads).
Total	10 to 12 hours

I leave the house at 10:00 p.m. and generally finish between 8:00 a.m. and 10:00 a.m., which leaves me available all day for family time and other interests. I do not sleep until Saturday night to get the feeling of being sleep deprived, which is important to train, especially in preparation for race day. I will do some phases of these workouts with other friends and some "solo" sessions for mental preparation.

Other ideas to consider: It's perfectly OK to miss a workout. My rule of thumb is that if you consistently perform 85 percent of all the workouts per week (as outlined in Chapter 4) you will be fine. Also, there will be many times when "life" gets crazy and your time will be limited. On those occasions,

I suggest you do a hard workout with intensity and miss the occasional long day. However, the key is to get in the long workouts each week if possible, as I outlined in Chapter 4. In this workout regime you include the back-to-back long days.

Another idea is to run or bike to a specific destination. If you have a family event, start early, and if it's reasonable based on location, time, and distance, then just meet the family there. Also, consider adding an early morning race as part of training. For example, if you are traveling to a wedding/event, and find the opportunity of a race close by, use this opportunity to train before the event.

As I mentioned, with some simple planning and a commitment, it's definitely possible to not quit your job and not be around your family to prepare for these long-distance races! Do keep in mind, I am married to my best friend, Jan who is also my greatest supporter and Super Crew. She also happens to be Greek. Those of you who have watched the famous movie "My Big Fat Greek Wedding," you have an idea of the massive entertaining that is common with large Greek families. So, with my heavy travel schedule, work, life and family responsibilities, constant entertaining and "being entertained" with the large

Greek family, we efficiently manage our time and schedules. Fortunately, we've also effectively combined our passions — of course, mine is racing in these events, and Jan loves to travel to experience new cultures and build new friendships. For us, a typical race located at a great destination combines our great loves. I race 30 hours and then enjoy "off-the-beaten-track" exploration of the country — and Jan gets her travel fix.

The best piece of advice I can impart: it's a balancing act with the most important part being your family time versus training and racing. You figure out effective time management tools that work for your individual situation; but you must make it a priority. You may also enlist the help of a coach to guide and assist you who knows the ins and outs of these races. Yes, I can help. Please contact me at wayne.kurtz@racetwitch.com.

CHAPTER 15 – ESSENTIAL TWITCH TIPS

Your comfort — especially on longer races — can make or break your enjoyment factor. It can also hinder your performance. In this chapter, we're going to provide some useful tips and tricks geared toward helping you achieve high degrees of comfort to not only improve your race time, but also enhance the entire experience.

An ongoing question we all face during long-distance endurance events relates to the compromise between weight and aerodynamics. Athletes want to know the value of lightweight shoes, bikes and clothing compared to gear that is less aerodynamic but more comfortable. Of course, in shorter events comfort becomes less of an issue (to some degree). In shorter events, athletes are more concerned regarding loss of speed related to wearing or not wearing socks during the run section of the triathlon or the value of changing clothes versus not changing clothes in the transition area.

These concerns change with longer events. As the race becomes significantly longer, comfort becomes more of issue for many of us. Being comfortable can counterbalance some of the intense fatigue that occurs in Ultra-Distance Triathlons. Here are few items to consider for your next ultra-distance event:

1. If you're competing in an Ultra-Distance Triathlon (Double, Triple, Quintuple, Deca events), the key is to stay on the bike and aerodynamics — especially races over the Double distance become less of a factor. Many athletes use lightweight road-bike geometry frames with aero bars and aero rims. The key is to STAY on the bike for as long as possible.

2. If you're racing the Deca distance race, consider using just a larger, somewhat heavier shoe to protect those toes during the later stages of the race when many athletes are prone to suffer with feet problems.

3. Consider using a two-piece wetsuit while swimming in the race. The advantage of the two-piece suit is that if chafing occurs or overheating, it's easy

to take off the top and keep the bottoms on and still have significant buoyancy from the legs, which tend to sink!

4. This tip is an absolute must in long-distance triathlons: make sure there are no seam problems in shorts, pants or shirts that will cause ongoing chafing.

5. Carry a small container of Glide, Bag Balm or other anti-friction cream in cycling shirt pockets or in your running pack during these long races.

6. For the very long bike section of an Ultra-Distance Triathlon (300-plus miles), consider using a fuel pack attached to the top tube, as it's very difficult after 20 hours or so to reach back to the pocket in your cycling jersey — I know this one well!

7. Fix your feet early before the "hot spots" become serious problems.

CONCLUSION

I hope you have found the information in *Beyond the Iron* helpful in your quest to learn about and eventually attempt an Ultra-Distance Triathlon in the future. What motivates me is giving to others and hearing the great positive, inspiring stories of individuals when they accomplish big goals. If you accomplish your goal of finishing one of the most difficult races in the world then my goals for you will be met.

As a passionate endurance athlete, I hope you can incorporate some of the methods/ideas that I have outlined in the book to further enhance your journey of completing one of these unique events.

Please don't hesitate to email me your thoughts (wayne.kurtz@racetwitch.com), race results and ideas. As I mentioned, I am a lifetime learner and am always interested in ideas to add to my personal training programs.

Wishing you all the best in your training and racing endeavors — and I hope to see you at a future race!

- Wayne Kurtz

World Records

Men			
Distance	Athlete	Record	Year/Race
Double	Huys	19 h 54 m 46 s	1993 Leuven*
Triple	Wildpanner	31 h 47 m 57 s	2003 Lehnsahn
Quadruple	Hojbjerre	53 h 41 m 00 s	1993 Hungary*
Quintuple	Conraux	73 h 18 m 16 s	2005 Monterrey
Deca	Lucas	192 h 08 m 26 s	1997 Monterrey

World Records

Women			
Distance	Athlete	Record	Year/Race
Double	Bischoff	22 h 07 m 00 s	1994 Huntsville
Triple	Benoehr	37 h 54 m 54 s	1996 Lensahn
Quadruple	Benoehr	59 h 15 m 00 s	1993 Hungary*
Quintuple	Benoehr	86 h 44 m 37 s	1994 Den Haag*
Deca	Andonie	249 h 14 m 52 s	1992 Monterrey

RESOURCES

2011 Races and Websites
IUTA Race schedule 2011

Date
Town
Country
Distance
Website
Remarks

04.02. – 05.02.2011
Playa Blanka
Lanzarote/Spain
Double World Cup Race
http://www.enduroman.com/

04.03. – 05.03.2011
Tampa
Florida/USA
Double World Cup Race
http://www.usaultratri.com/

10.06. – 12.06.2011
Neulengbach
Austria
Double World Championship
http://www.triathlon-neulengbach.at/

08.07. – 10.07.2011
Bonyhad
Hungary
Double World Cup Race
http://www.ultraironhungary.com/

28.07. – 31.07.2011
Lensahn
Germany
Triple World Cup Race
http://www.triathlonlensahn.de/

06.08. – 08.08.2011
Lichtfield
United Kingdom
Double World Cup Race
http://www.enduroman.com/

27.08. – 29.08.2011
Murska Sobota
Slovenia
Double World Cup Race
http://www.triatlon-ms.si/

08.09. – 11.09.2011
Frauenfeld
Switzerland
Double World Cup Race
http://www.ultratriathlon.ch/

07.10. – 09.10.2011
Lake Anna
Virginia USA
Double World Cup Race
http://www.usaultratri.com/

07.11. – 17.11.2011
Monterrey
Mexico
Deca Iron World Cup Race
http://www.multisport.com.mx/

IUTA Website
http://www.iutasport.com

APPENDIX

WAYNE'S ULTRA-DISTANCE TRIATHLON TOP 65 ITEMS – RACE CHECKLIST

1. Wetsuit and additional wetsuit(s) for crew (if they wade into the water for providing fuel/food)
2. Two pairs of goggles
3. Swimming suit
4. Swim cap (in the event the water is very cold)
5. Two to five pairs of biking shorts (I prefer bib-cycling shorts for very long races)
6. Two to five cycling shirts
7. Two to five pairs running shorts
8. Two to five short sleeve race shirts for run
9. One tank top racing shirt for run
10. Two long sleeve wicking shirts
11. Eight pairs of running/biking socks – consider wool

12. Two pairs of compression socks
13. Two running hats
14. Bag Balm – or other cream to use on feet or very chafed areas
15. Anti-chafing lubricant/creams
16. Cooking spray (for your ankles when putting on the wetsuit – makes it easy to slide off)
17. Duct Tape (plenty of it – used for blisters, holds things together, a must!)
18. Knife
19. Band aids
20. Lip balm
21. Sunscreen
22. One can Dragon Balm or other balm for very sore muscles
23. Arm warmers/leg warmers
24. Cycling gloves/ winter cycling gloves for night if it's cold
25. Bike-shoe covers
26. Lightweight rain jacket
27. One cycling and one running warm jacket
28. Two to three pairs of running shoes (for the Deca, plan on at least three pairs each a ½ size larger for swollen feet)
29. Two pair of cycling shoes (if you break a cleat on the shoes, always have a replacement)
30. Bike – if you can drive to the race (take extra set

of wheels or additional bike so you don't have to waste time changing flat tires)

31. Bike pump
32. One bike helmet (consider an aero helmet as well)
33. Five to six bike water bottles (can never have enough bike bottles!)
34. Small Bento Box for the bike to hold food
35. Four sets of headlamps for bike and transition area
36. One set of flasher lights for bike
37. Specific energy drink – food (Hammer Perpeteum for me)
38. Spoon and bowl to mix energy drink so it can be put in small gel flasks
39. Favorite gels (multiple flavors)
40. Gel flasks
41. Running race belt/flask holder
42. Two water-bottle holders for run
43. Electrolyte drink if you don't know or like what the race offers
44. Energy bars
45. Peanut butter, Nutella (of course, races will provide various food items for all athletes and crews)
46. Hammer products: Endurolytes, Race Caps, Anti-Fatigue Caps, Premium Insurance Caps
47. Two Endurolyte "coin holders"

48. Sunglasses
49. Extra seat bracket for bike (in the event you break the seat bracket screw by over-tightening — yes, this has happened to me)
50. Allen wrenches, pedal wrench and tool bag for bike
51. First-aid kit
52. Five pre-stretched tubular bike tires or multiple tubes if you're using clinchers
53. Bike oil
54. Backpack
55. Three to five garbage bags
56. Various assortment of sandwich and plastic bags
57. REI one-minute coffee maker
58. Propane stove
59. Rope to hang clothes/pliers
60. Country flag – to display and run through the finish line with
61. Tent/sleeping bag/ pillow/ground cloth (especially for longer Ultra-Distance Triathlons)
62. Two chairs if not supplied by the race
63. iPod or MP3 player (if you use them during a race)
64. Race strategy written – laminated card
65. Wine to drink for your crew!

MORE RESOURCES OR TO ORDER PRODUCTS

If you would like to order more books or products, visit our website, www.beyondtheiron.com, and see author videos, blog and resources.

We also have other wonderful resources you can subscribe to by logging onto the website at http://www.racetwitch.com, which is the world's largest race resource for multiple disciplines.

Check out RacePeak.com — your trusted endurance sports advisor to assist you in having an exceptional racing season — guaranteed!

Subscribe to Endurance Racing Report at http:/www.enduranceracingreport.com.

WAYNE KURTZ

I have a lifelong passion of racing in various endurance sport races throughout the world. I continue to search for unique races to add to my race calendar each year. At the time of this writing, 2010 is my silver anniversary of racing (25 years). My specific interests include, triathlons, running races, cycling races, and snowshoeing racing at various distances. I'm also interested in ultra-distance events: Double, Quintuple, Deca Ironman, 100-mile and multi-day running events. The events, traveling memories and lifelong friendships that I have experienced through the endurance-racing community, has been so valuable in my life.

The ongoing challenge we all experience is finding specific races throughout the world within each of our racing interests in one resource/website. The normal process is to search various websites, magazines and Google for specific races. The result is a time-consuming process of searching. The goal of my company, RaceTwitch.com, is to provide a solution to this "searching" problem. It is the online resource for the worldwide endurance community that provides one location to search and evaluate specific races within distinct disciplines. The uniqueness of RaceTwitch.com is the functionality of sharing registered users' feedback from race reviews and specific recommended races based upon their interests and racing profile.

I want to share with the worldwide endurance sports racing community a value-based, user friendly race resource to enhance their experiences.

WEBER COUNTY LIBRARY
3 1301 01491 6204